I0786124

Paying for Sex:
A Global Guide to Prostitution

Rockit Reports

CONTENTS

I. Paying for It

Prostitution is commonly said to be the oldest profession in existence. Whether or not that is true is a question experts have wrangled over for years. Who exactly is an expert? It would depend on who you ask.

Some have called me an expert on the subject. I hesitate to accept the classification, even if I have reported extensively on the commercial sex industry around the world for many years.

In any event I do know some things about the subject, and I'll share them with you over the following pages.

The sex is a thriving component of the world economy, operating everywhere from the most cosmopolitan urban centers in the richest countries to the most out of the way sections of the most underdeveloped places.

Is it okay for men to offer money to women in exchange for sexual services? The answers given to that question are as varied as the reasons women enter the trade to begin with. Quite frankly, it's not for me to judge. Although I am for the full decriminalization of the practice, I am simply a reporter.

Why do men pay for sex? Again the reasons are varied. Perhaps the most common answer would be that it is the easiest way for many men to find a quick sexual liaison with no strings attached. When asked by a judge why he resorted to paying women for sex when he could find so many women to have sex with him for free, the American actor Charlie Sheen famously remarked: "I don't pay them for sex. I pay them to leave!"

The ethical questions behind sex work and indeed the current state of commerce in general are many, and outside of the scope of this book. "Paying for Sex" simply aims to explain things as they actually are. Questions as to the philosophy of sex work are best left for other volumes, or perhaps even other authors.

I for one don't think that the commercial sex industry is a shameful topic. It is something that abounds, creating untold income all around the world. Doesn't that alone prove that is something we should examine? At the very least we should be free to discuss it.

One day I hope we'll all be free enough from the social constraints we impose upon ourselves for various reasons to simply engage with each other for purposes of sexual pleasure on the basis of mutual agreement attraction. Unfortunately, at the moment, that's not always possible. So we find ourselves here.

In my years on this earth I've traveled near and far, covering the sex industry all around the world in print and on the internet in the process. For better or worse I have become quite knowledgeable about the global sex trade.

I wrote this with the intention of sharing what I know for the benefit of whoever is interested in reading it. It serves as an updated and expanded volume building on much shorter workers published long ago.

It should be obvious that I do not advocate that anyone violate the laws in place anywhere in the world. In fact, I don't advocate anything at all. This book was created for no other reason than to entertain the reader. Act at your own discretion and remember that "your mileage may vary."

II. Learning About It

I must assume that nearly every adult knows what prostitution is. As one of the oldest industries in human society it is also one of the most well known. But how many outside of actual participants in the global sex trade know the ins and outs?

Depending on your background you may be surprised to learn about many aspects of the industry, either in your neck of the woods or in other parts of the world.

There are millions of people engaged in the sale of sexual services. They come from all over and although there are some generalities, things can vary greatly from one town to another.

A wide variety of sexual services is offered in exchange for cash in all sorts of establishments, or in some cases, in apartments or even vehicles.

In the coming pages I will describe the most common sexual services for sale around the world, along with the kinds of places in which they are typically offered.

You may learn a lot, or you may just confirm what you already know. Either way I trust you will find it engaging.

1. Compensated Dating

Compensated dating, which goes on under any variety of labels including the "sugar daddy" relationship, is probably one of the most common types of sexual services offered around the world today.

Depending on how you classify things, it may even be possible to say that most prostitution in the world takes place in this sort of scenario.

What is compensated dating? Simply put, it is the exchange of money for a certain amount of a woman's time, during which she will often – but not always – provide sexual services. Things are not always done on a purely formal and commercial basis. For example, a guy may fork over a certain amount of money to a woman each month with the understanding that the two will have sex somewhat regularly. The woman involved doesn't hand over an itemized invoice charging X amount of money for a particular number of sessions.

Compensated comes in many forms. In some places it has been a common practice for ages. In others it seems to losing popularity. Still there are other places where the newest generation to come to adulthood is heavily engaged in the practice.

Compensated dating probably first came into the public consciousness when reports of it emerged from parts of Asia like Tokyo and Hong Kong. Later it seemed to spread to various parts of the world. In reality, relationships between moneyed up men and their "kept women" have existed for as long as money has existed.

The kept woman and mistress still exists, now alongside

a growing number of "sugar babies" who rely on the "donations" of their sponsors. Sometimes this goes on for years. Other times it boils down to a single meeting that would could easily mistake for a client's rendezvous with an escort.

There are countless college students and others of the same age who meet men online. When they once used websites like Craigslist, things have changed. Now they use anything from specialized sugar baby websites to mainstream smart phone applications like Tinder to seek out sponsors.

Most of these women are not full time sex workers, and couldn't really be labeled pros since they don't rely solely on sex work for income. They are just using what they have available to them to pick up a little extra money. This sort of meeting also happens elsewhere.

In Colombia, there are who called *prepagados* who meet guys in nightclubs and similar places then date them and more in exchange for money. It isn't as obvious as a pay for play transaction but essentially that is what is happening.

In Japan, there are countless clubs set up specifically for women to meet men willing to pay for their time. They range from places like the many Kirari Community Cafes that specialize in one off meetings to elaborate fully staffed agencies like Universe Club that allow male members to search through massive databases of willing and available women.

Of course there are full timers. These are women who expect to meet all of their financial needs through money given to them by men with money. They look for one or more sponsor to pay for their housing, food, clothing and other expenses. In exchange, they offer company. Typically they make sex available too, though again that is not even the case. There are even some women who purposely deny sex to their sponsors and even humiliate them. They cater to guys with a somewhat uncommon fetish known as financial domination or "fin dom."

Escorts and their customers could even be described as

practicing compensated dating. In many cases the way escorts get around laws against prostitution while still advertising publicly is to say that they only charge for their company, not for any sexual activities. Of course most escorts do offer sexual services in private, and it is widely considered a standard part of their service. Absurd regulations can lead people to take absurd actions.

There are also women who work in hostess bars who could be described as offering a sort of compensated dating. These women offer company, service, and kindness to men who buy them overpriced drinks. They are usually under no obligation to leave with a customer. But if they chose to depart with one for a predetermined amount, sex is usually in the cards. It's not uncommon for guys to take hostess bar workers out of bars for extended periods of time. Often this "boyfriend girlfriend" relationship involves the exchange of money too.

Hostess bars are most common in Asia, but variations on the theme do exist in other parts of the world. I'll describe hostess bars in more detail later.

The above gives an idea of the various kinds of compensated dating that exists. Of course compensated dating is not limited to what was written. It can take on other forms as well.

What separates compensated dating from other kinds of sex work is that it usually involves more of an affectionate feel, or at least the pretense of such. Whether or not it is genuine is up for debate and probably depends on the situation. There can be no doubt that some clients have fallen in love with prostitutes, and the same also occurs in reverse though it is not nearly as common.

It is a fact that at least some of the women who participate in this kind of work may consider the actual cash payment they receive to be a bonus for something that enjoy doing. For example, some may like to be taken out on the town, or to have an excuse to have a wide variety of sexual partners in a world where women who do are often looked down upon publicly. Some may hope to find a wealthy gentleman to take them away from wherever they find themselves. For such women financial compensations could just be a cherry on top. I'm absolutely sure that this doesn't apply to every woman who participates in compensated dating, but it does apply to others nonetheless.

For whatever reason, women who do this kind of work are usually not as hardened as some of the women who participate in the more mechanical, openly commercial aspects of the trade. There are always exceptions.

2. Erotic Massage

Human beings have quite a history with massage. Long used as a way to relieve stress and cure illness, it has also become a thinly-veiled cover for prostitution in many places. Sometimes the sexual services are tied in with genuine massage services, as much a way to make even more money as an attempt at making sure customers are truly relieved. Even without a financial component, erotic massage appears in a variety of forms going way back into our past.

The motivations masseuses have for providing sexual services today vary widely, from the tantric practitioner who believes stroking the "lingam" is a standard part of massage to the broke Chinese immigrant who sees no harm in massaging a penis rather than a toe if it will triple her salary in a matter of seconds. There are also "massage parlors" that offer little or no massage at all and simply serve as brothels in disguise.

The wide variety of options in the massage world is probably too extensive for me to cover without throwing off the balance of the whole book. I am after all writing about the trade as a whole, not simply erotic massage. For those interested, I have published an entire volume focusing only on this aspect of the commercial sex industry called "Happy Ending Massage: The Complete Report."

Most erotic massage parlors are more or less hidden in plain sight. In some countries like Thailand they may have women in sexy clothes sitting in front of the shop and menus that list services like "bareback blow job" In places like the United States where the authorities are more strict and quick to clamp down on erotic massage establishments, interested men looking for happy endings check the internet for reviews of places or seek out massage parlors with blocked out windows and business hours that extend well into the early morning.

Services and prices can vary widely. Everything from low end "jack shacks" where men receive hand jobs for a few dollars in tiny cubicles to giant soapy massage parlor complexes that resemble five star hotels and staff magazine models who provide full sex can be found by those who know where to look.

In coming chapters I will describe the most common types of massage parlors and providers that offer sexual services for money. Things change from one country and group of practitioners to the next, but there is a surprising amount of uniformity that transcends it all.

3. Brothels

Brothels are exactly what they sound like. There's a reason they are colloquially known as "whore houses." Essentially they are places that house sex workers who service customers for money.

What makes a place a brothel rather than something else – for instance an "erotic spa" – is up for debate. There are those who describe any place offering sexual services as a brothel. For the purposes of this book I think an attempt at defining a brothel is in order.

A brothel is a place where customers walk in and have sexual relations with a sex worker more or less on demand. It matters not if the customer can select a sex worker of his choosing. The main criteria is that the place offers sexual intercourse in exchange for money with little more in between.

Places that offer things like genuine full body massages with a chance or even a guarantee of erotic services are not brothels then. They are erotic massage parlors.

By the same token, the barbershop fronts in a country like South Korea who have sex with customers for money soon after meeting would be brothels. Other barbershops in Asia where legitimate salon services are offered with some female staff offering erotic extras like hand jobs in addition would not be considered brothels.

Places that openly consider themselves as brothels such as the famous (and legal) Moonlight Bunny Ranch near Las Vegas are obviously such. The same goes for places like Agentur Liberty in Berlin.

This seems like the most reasonable way to define a

brothel to me. But I am clearly not the deciding force on the question. Others will continue to call any place with sex workers inside a brothel, and ultimately they may not be wrong.

4. Red Light Districts

Red light districts are another sort of place that is broadly defined by a lot of people. Some consider any place where sex workers ply their trade to be a red light district. I do not. I think that a red light district is a particular kind of place with a certain mode of operation.

Without question, the most famous example of an actual red light district would be De Wallen in Amsterdam. At De Wallen, sex workers wait in windows trying to attract guys who pass by. If a guy is intrigued he enters a sex worker's room and negotiates a price. If both parties agree, the window is closed and the sex worker and client do what they've just agreed upon in a private part of the room in back.

Of course prostitution is legal in the Netherlands, so the De Wallen red light district is well known. Others follow the same sort of model. That includes the nearby Singelgebied and De Pijp red light districts as well as the more distant Bahnhofsviertel in Frankfurt.

In South Korea prostitution is officially illegal but you would never know that after walking through any of the many red light districts there such as Miarai Texas or Cheonho in Seoul. They have the same sort of big windows filled with women as De Wallen in Amsterdam.

Although it operates on a slightly different model with women standing in the street and using more private quarters, I would also include Bogota's Santa Fe in any list of red light districts around the world.

Such a list would not however include the row of hostess bars on Street 104 in Phnom Penh, which I will discuss later, or even the row of open short time bars filled with scantly clad women on Soi 6 in Pattaya which will also get a mention.

While the services rendered are usually more or less the same around the world, prices can vary between red light districts or even between individual women in particular places. Still some market rates are usually established. For example in De Wallen twenty minutes is typically 50 Euros ($57 USD) while in Sante Fe the same amount of time is normally 40,000 Pesos ($13 USD).

In general, red light districts seem to be on the way out around the world. A combination of crackdowns and disinterest from guys more involved in internet use seems to be behind it all. Cheongnyangni 588 in Seoul has been mostly demolished. Even De Wallen is now much smaller than it used to be and there are plans in the works to reduce its size even further in the near future.

5. Blow Job Bars

Although it may come to a surprise to some who struggle in life to find a woman to provide them with oral sex on a regular basis, blow job bars of one form or another are actually quite common in many countries around the world. In some places they're even discussed and joked about openly on television!

Though they have some commonalities that stretch across borders, blow job bars also have their differences at both the individual and nation levels. Here I will try to explain how blow job bars work in the various places they commonly exist.

A blow job bar is exactly what it sounds like: a bar where guys can go to get a blow job. Of course a fee is charged, and typically it is set the same for everyone.

These places are most often referred to as blow job bars, but they can also be called BJ bars, hands free bars, pink salons, pinsaros, or blow job barbershops. As some of those names would indicate, blow job bars are not always actually located in bars. Many of them don't serve alcohol at all.

So why the name "blow job bar?" I can't be sure, but my guess is that English speakers mostly commonly come in contact with the BJ bar model of suck shop. These are most common in Thailand which is one of the countries most often visited by English speakers. The many BJ bars in Thailand are oriented to foreigners to the point that most won't even accept Thai customers. Blow job barbershops in Vietnam and pink salons in Japan are even more plentiful, but oriented to locals. They aren't seen or visited by English speaking foreigners nearly as much. In Japan, many of them won't even accept foreigners as customers.

Thai blow job bars exist mainly in the cities most visited by foreigners. That would be Bangkok and Pattaya. At least BJ bar existed in the beach town of Hua Hin but that seems to have closed.

In the Thai bars the women on staff typically wait in front of the venue or just inside. When customers walk in they select one of the women on staff or simply take whoever is next in line. Then they move to either a private booth or a chair right out in the open, though the open operations are becoming more rare. Next the customers drop their pants and have the genitals cleaned either in a sink or with a damp cloth. That is followed by oral sex that typically lasts until the customer has an orgasm. The prices for this range from 600 to 1000 Baht ($18-30 USD). Most ask for 700 or 900 Baht. As far as I know only Wood Bar, formerly known as the world famous Dr BJ's, charges a full thousand Baht for the service.

In Japan blow job bars are even more common though they rarely exist in actual bars. Instead these "pink salons" are set up in places that almost resemble a cafe. That's fitting too since customers are usually given a glass of tea with their admission fee of 3000 to 7000 Yen ($27 – 63 USD). In most cases foreigners are not admitted.

Pink salons are often referred to locally as "pinsaro" which is just a Japanese way of saying the same thing. While the light are often kept low these places don't offer much privacy. The rooms are open and customers can rather clearly see the service providers blowing customers around the room. It's not uncommon for the providers to get fully nude or even do a 69 position in the little booths.

The providers who work the pinsaros range in looks but probably skew towards the older and those who might not do as well in other parts of the commercial sex industry. These kinds of places are not known for attracting the best looking women in Japan.

On the other hand, women working the so-called lip cafes in South Korea do tend to be quite attractive. Many women in their twenties take up the work for whatever reason. Despite the name, the places themselves aren't really like cafes at all. Instead they operate out of apartment or massage parlor like complexes in the upper levels of buildings. They advertise discreetly online and often screen their customers.

In private rooms inside these lip cafes customers are given twenty minutes of time with one of the women on staff. Services vary but kissing and oral sex is common. Prices are usually around 35,000 Won ($32 USD) but can go up from there if things like mutual oral are involved. Most lip cafes in Korea do not accept foreign customers, especially if they can't speak the local language.

Vietnam is home to many blow job barbershops. These places pose as barbershops or hair washing salons for men in order to get around restrictions against sex work. Most reports seem to indicate that the authorities are aware of these places but lack either the will or ability to stop them.

Blow job barbershops exist all over Vietnam but for whatever reason they are much more common in Ho Chi Minh City than Hanoi.

Vietnamese blow job barbershops are staffed by anywhere from a few to a few dozen women. They can vary greatly in looks. Some places hire very attractive women in their early 20's while others may only have one or two much older women on staff. In many shops the women wear matching uniforms consisting of things like low cut tops and short tight skirts.

When customers enter these blow job barbershops they select one of the women on staff then head to a semi-private cubicle or room. The private areas are usually located on upper floors and behind locked doors. Each space contains a narrow massage table and a sink ostensibly meant for washing hair.

Next they take of their shirt and shoes. Finally they lay down on the massage table face up. Next their service provider pulls their pants down and cleans their genitals and hands. The sink which is normally stocked with soap is used for that.

Finally the main service is performed. As the name would suggest blow jobs are rendered. They often come along with all sorts of erotic activity that can include things like kisses all over the body, oral performed with an ice cub or hot tea in the mouth, or even analingus (also known as "rimming").

In many cases the service providers lower their tops and take off their panties so customers can touch or at least see their bodies. In some cases they even crawl on the table and perform in the 69 position. It all depends on the place, the customer and even the provider.

Prices on the other hand don't vary much between blow job barbershops in Vietnam. Most charge right around 200,000 Dong ($8.50 USD) per session. Customers typically tip between 100,000 and 200,000 Dong more directly to their service providers.

Blow job barbershops are numerous in Vietnam but they obviously don't advertise themselves as suck shops. Instead they use other little hints to bring in customers. Overall they are generally somewhat quite and out of the main lines of sight of most unassuming individuals.

There are also many more mainstream barbershops and hair salons for men in Vietnam that do not offer sexual services of any kind. Counter-intuitively these places often have some of the most beautiful women on staff, dressed in somewhat revealing outfits and exposed to passersby on the streets.

There are at least two bars aimed at foreigners in Vietnam where women on staff offer blow jobs on premises. The women are in their thirties or older typically and a bit hardened. The main customer base seems to be horny or perhaps somewhat unaware foreign guys who are sucked off in semi-private booths for as much as $100 in US currency.

The capital city of Cambodia was previously home to two blow job bars where customers could get blown right at the bar at least for a little while for around one US dollar. Many male visitors got into the habit of trying the service from all the women available. Both of these bars have disappeared from the scene however and now the days of blow jobs in bars are limited to secretive activities in the dark corners of just a handful of venues.

Hong Kong still has one bar that could be called a blow job bar bar in the Wan Chai section of the main island. It's actually more of a go go bar where women from Southeast Asia dance on stage in bikinis. Customers who enter are led to one of two corner booths where another lady on staff gives them oral in exchange for drinks that cost the equivalent of $32 US while an older dragon lady style mamasan oversees it all.

Blow jobs aren't the focus at the bar however. Mirrors on the wall allow customers to see the stage while they are being serviced. The goal seems to be to get the guys aroused and intrigued by the women on stage to the point that they agree to pay 1500 Hong Kong Dollars ($191 USD) to take a dancer out of the bar for sex.

Theoretically, the women who work at blow job bars should be better at giving head than most others. This is often the case, but sometimes it simply isn't. It depends on any number of factors. As a general rule it seems that most of the women who work the venues in Thailand and Vietnam are quite skilled. At the same time, ladies working similar shops in Japan and Hong Kong don't have the same sort of reputation. Of course there are always exceptions.

Why do women work in BJ bars? The numbers are numerous. More than a few want access to quick cash but don't want to be seen in public with their customers, often because they're in a serious relationship or even married.

Blow job bars can also be a place for women deemed too unattractive or old to work elsewhere in the sex industry or even younger or more attractive gals in need of a quick buck.

Surprisingly, the women working at blow job shops in nearly every country they exist tend to be quite friendly. More than one visitor has commented that gals in a Thai blow job bar were much more friendly than the often hardened strippers they've encountered in western countries like the United States.

This all gives a general idea of what blow job bars are like around the world, even if it doesn't explain everything. It's beyond the scope of this book to delve too far into the ins and outs of every blow job bar around , but for those who are interested in the subject I have published an in-depth volume on professional penis polishing pubs entitled "Blow Job Bars: The Complete Report."

6. Hostess Bars

You'll remember that I mentioned hostess bars earlier in the compensated dating section. While what goes on in hostess bars could probably be considered a form of compensated dating, hostess bars are prominent and unique enough to deserve their own description.

Hostess bars are sometimes also called girl bars, beer bars, girlie bars, or g pubs. They're basically bars staffed by women who spend time inside with customers. That time can be used doing anything from just talking to dancing, playing pool or playing a game like Connect Four.

Women working in hostess bars make money in a few ways. First they get a flat salary. On top of that they make commission on each of the "lady drinks" purchased for them. Guys normally purchase lady drinks for any women they want to spend time with. The lady drinks cost the same or a little more than drinks for customers. The ladies get a cut of the total price.

Depending on local customs, the customers may also tip the hostesses directly for their time. For example it's common for customers at hostess bars in Ho Chi Minh City to give ladies a tip for spending time with them.

What goes down in these kinds of places differs depending on their locations, local rules and practices, the staff, the customers, and in some cases even the time of the year a customer visits.

In some cases the women who work in hostess bars will go out of the bars with customers. In other cases they won't. Most women fall somewhere in between, going out of the bar with some customers but not with others. Not even woman who goes out of the bar is going to have sex with a customer but most probably do.

Some of the women in some of the hostess bars are in the habit of getting quite touchy with customers. Some are even known to pull penises out of pants so they can tug or suck on them. Others won't even touch customers in any circumstance.

Some women working in hostess bars are married or even virgins who will not have sex with customers even if they do leave the bar. There are all sorts of variations.

Normally when a guy takes a woman out of a hostess bar he pays a bar fine. Theoretically this is meant to compensate the bar for its loss of staff and the salary it paid out. Some say its actually a way for bars to further profit from the interactions between the customers and ladies.

Hostess bars don't always take the shape of bars even if that is the most common format. Hostess bars, or maybe more accurately "hostess clubs," come in the form of bars closed in behind frosted glass doors, private cafes, outdoor beer bars, karaoke rooms, car washes, and more.

The typical hostess bar format is most common in places like Vietnam and Cambodia. The Cambodian hostess bars actually seem to be based on the Vietnamese bars which would make sense considering recent history.

In Vietnam there are mainly two types of hostess bars. In one there is no bar fine system and customers just spend time with the ladies inside unless they can form some kind of relationship after hours. In the other type there is a semi-secretive bar fine system in place and the hostess will have sex with customers for money in some cases. In the places that do bar fines, customers usually pay around the equivalent of 80 US dollars for a short round of sex with a hostess.

In Cambodia everything depends on the women. Pretty much every hostess bar has a bar fine with the possible exception of one or two. It's up to the ladies themselves to decide if they want to go out with a customer. Those who do usually expect anywhere from 30 to 100 US dollars for their time and effort.

In parts of Thailand there are some "G-pubs" along with several "beer bars." G-pubs are basically high end closed versions of hostess bars that may charge membership fees. Beer bars are open air bars staffed by women who more or less act like hostesses in other forms of the business.

A type of hostess bar is also common in Japan, where it's called a "girl's bar" or "snack bar," and South Korea, where it's called a "juicy bar." In those countries the hostesses usually just drink and play games with customers. Bar fines are rare if they exist at all. In most of Japan's girl bars, the women are strictly prohibited from touching customers.

In many parts of Asia there are other forms of hostess bars that range from the kyabakura of Japan to the KTVs of China and Taiwan. Prices are typically on the higher end of things and the women on staff try their best to entertain the customers. In a lot of cases there is no sex offered but in some Karaoke clubs it is actually the norm. Again it depends on local rules and practices.

A version of the kyabakura for women also exists in Japan, where it is in fact quite popular. In the "host bars" men are compensated for spending time with women and making them feel loved. Actual sex is apparently uncommon but it does occur in some cases. A form of this host bar business also exists in South Korea and Thailand in more limited form.

7. Spas, Saunas and Entertainment Complexes

One model of commercial sex venue that is common around the world is the male sauna. They go by different names and range in size and exact procedures, but all of the male sex saunas follow a similar pattern.

These venues could be roughly categorized into four different models. There are the FKK saunas, the Chinese saunas, the Chinese spas, and the male entertainment complexes.

FKK saunas are based in Europe. They seem to have originated in the German-speaking areas. FKK is a German acronym for the phrase *freikörperkultur*. This translates to "free body culture" and has roots going far back in history. In the context of the commercial sex industry it is used to describe sex shops loosely based on a nudist club model.

Basically female sex workers go to a FKK to find customers. They pay an admission fee which grants them full access to the grounds. Once inside they walk around either in the nude or in sexy lingerie. Male customers pay an admission fee to enter as well. That gives them access to the place as well, along with free drinks and food. The men normally wear robes.

The service providers and men are free to mingle and make arrangements for sex in private rooms or public areas such as theaters where porno is played on big screens.

FKK saunas exist in Germany, Austria, the Czech Republic, and Switzerland. The FKK clubs are usually large and have things like buffets, bars, lounges, swimming pools and outdoor areas. Entrance fees are usually between 50 and 90

Euros ($58-104 USD). Sex is typically sold for between 50 and 60 Euros.

Chinese saunas are large venues where male customers are king. Some have even described them as "a male paradise."

These saunas have a wide range of facilities inside including things like pools, hot tubs, buffets, private rooms, massage rooms and table massages.

Customers pay a fee to enter. After that they are treated to as many services as they care to pay for. They can be showered by women who give them a bit of oral sex when they enter. After that they can get hair cuts, body massage, manicures, pedicures, ear cleanings, foot massages and famously "thigh massages" which are more or less extended penis and testicle massages designed to make customers feel great pleasure without ejaculating.

Food and drink runs freely and customers can typically get as much of both as they'd like. They can also watch any of the large modern televisions or simply take a snooze in large recliner style lounge chairs. Staff abounds to wait on them hand and foot.

The main service sold is full sex with one or more of the many beautiful women on staff. These ladies walk around in lingerie and line up for customers who want to book a session. The ladies who are Chinese, Vietnamese, Thai, Russian, Central Asian, Korea, or even African, are typically experts at sexual services. They provide everything from full body kisses to rimming and sex to their customers in private rooms that could fit in any four star hotel.

Prices range in the saunas but aren't as expensive as some might imagine, assuming they can even imagine that such places actually exist. A guy who spends the equivalent of $400 US in a mid-sized sauna could expect to be bathed, fed, massaged, cleaned, masturbated and ridden to orgasm over a six to twelve hour period.

Chinese saunas are most common in Macau where sex work is legal. Chinese saunas also exist in mainland China though they operate on a more underground level and are subject to closure at any time. The southern Chinese city of Dongguan was once filled with sex saunas. Today the scene has mostly been destroyed or "cleaned up" depending on how you look at it.

Chinese spas are smaller places where the focus is more typically on sex. These places are often labeled as spas or health centers. Some are called saunas too. I describe these places as Chinese spas though they might not consider themselves as such. Still the name seems to fit the model.

While the Chinese style saunas are filled with all sorts of things from comfortable lounges to swimming facilities, the spas are usually much smaller and more moderate. The facilities are rarely spectacular and many customers simply do without them all together. In some cases the facilities are more for show than anything else.

Its common for customers to rock up to these types of places and simply ask for a lineup of the women on staff. They are then shown the women working the spa one by one or in a group. If they choose one of the women they head off to a private room where they typically receive erotic services. The women are usually Chinese, Vietnamese, Thai, Indonesian or occasionally Malay, Colombian, or even Russian.

These spas are more common in Indonesia, Singapore, and Malaysia. Prices vary depending on the place, but it's common for customers to pay around the equivalent of $100 US for a session that includes sex.

Male entertainment complexes are large buildings with multiple floors where all sorts of things go on. They normally have nightclubs inside that are frequented by working women, more private club areas where dancers work poles and sometimes the poles of customers too, and large saunas where male customers can spend alone time with sexy women from around the world.

Male entertainment saunas can range from the amazingly cheap to the surprisingly expensive. They are typically visited by well off locals but foreigners don't ever seem to be turned away on account of their national origins. Customers can spend anywhere from the equivalent of $50 to $5000 US dollars in these complexes depending on the place and what exactly they get up to.

These complexes are most common in Indonesia with most located in the capital city of Jakarta. Although the complexes are large and well established there are signs things could be changing.

The famous Alexis Hotel with its large club and sauna was recently hit with allegations of facilitating prostitution by the new city government. The sauna section of the building was closed. There is talk that things will go further and touch other establishments too. No one knows for sure what is to come.

Male sex saunas exist in one form or another in many countries around the world. There are well-known places like the large Artemis sauna in the middle of Berlin, much smaller out of the way places tucked into side alleys and hotel basements in Kuala Lumpur, and everything in between.

I have given you a general description of this type of venue here. The local varieties of male sex sauna will be described in more detail later.

8. Strip Clubs

The American comedian Chris Rock once put out a hit song warning that "no matter what a stripper tells you, there is no sex in the champagne room." That's probably correct in most cases, as strippers like juicy bar girls in Korea, lead customers on to make more money. But sex is sold in strip clubs.

In a lot of strip clubs in the US, customers aren't even allowed to touch the dancers. Still in some places all sorts of deals are cut.

There are totally above ground places like the corporate-owned Rick's Cabaret chain where dancers wouldn't offer anything extra in almost all cases, but even there you can bet that some performers are cutting side deals with moneyed up guys to meet outside of the bar. I personally of know at least two dancers from major corporate clubs who have met rich customers after work from time to time for a little pay for play.

Then there are the places where extras are common even right in the clubs. Usually this consists of stuff like mutual massage or condom covered blow jobs in the VIP rooms. At one large strip club in a rural part of the US, new customers are commonly given a sort of menu run down as soon as they enter. There sex is sold for $300 in a back room and hand jobs are offered for $80 for those who don't want to spend as much or go all the way.

Finally there are the many dancers who just do their own thing and meet customers for money or help them out in dark corners of the bars. It's not going on with every dancer at every bar by any means, but it does go on.

Then there are the strip clubs in other countries where prostitution is either allowed or tolerated in some form. Many punters tell stories of groping dancers and much more in Toronto strip clubs. In Austria and the Czech Republic dancers work the poles on the stages along with the poles carry in their pants.

At AAA Exclusive Club in Prague the dancers don't normally take off their clothes on stage, but they do regularly have sex with customers in private rooms upstairs for 2000 Koruna ($89 USD) per twenty minute session.

The women at Maxim in Vienna don't often get their clothes off either. They don't even dance on the stage as much as you might expect. At the same time, they regularly have sex with customers in private quarters on club premises for 120 Euro ($137 USD).

Fase II is a very well known strip club in Medellin, Colombia with a huge staff of ladies. The dancers all work the stage in various states of undress and sell sex in the private cabana rooms next door for 190,000 Pesos ($63 USD). At Conejita's in the same city dancers commonly sell sex for 80,000 Pesos ($27 USD).

Sex is sold openly in plenty of strip clubs in Tijuana too. The same goes for the clubs that come as close as the Dominican Republic gets to strip clubs, even if most foreigners don't even know the places exist.

Still other strip clubs around the world follow more of a US model or worse. At Tantra Tokyo in Japan for example there is no sex offered at all even though sexual services are widely available throughout the country. In Eastern Europe there are countless horror stories of customers being scammed out of all sorts of money in strip joints.

So sometimes there is sex in the champagne room, or outside of it. Sometimes there is just dancing. There are no hard and fast rules that apply everywhere and all the time. In some places, there are no rules at all except maybe the rule of the jungle!

9. Go Go Bars or "A-Go-Gos"

There are go go bars and then there are "go go bars." In some parts of the US, strip clubs where women don't actually strip but instead dance around in short shorts and bikini tops are called go go bars. Sex is rarely sold in these remnant of the 1960's so they don't need to be discussed any further here.

The topic of discussion here are the many go go bars spread across Southeast Asia. They exist in Thailand and the Philippines and are common in some cities more than others. For example, the mountain city of Chiang Mai in Thailand has just three go go bars while the beach city of Pattaya in the same country has dozens.

While go go bars vary from one place to the next with some having fully nude dancers and others having dancers in shorts, shirts and even stockings, some things do remain the same.

The women in go go bars generally dance in order to show themselves to the customers. The hope is that the customers will pay a bar fine to take them out of the bar. That usually means there will be an exchange of money for sex which ultimately it is the point of the whole thing. Because of this, some may even despairingly refer to go go bars as "meat markets" if they were so inclined.

Go go bars range from the small hole-in-the-wall to the large multi-level building complete with huge stages and professional lighting and sound. Some gogos are reserved places while others are wild places where naked women and horny men interact physically in front of everyone. I have already laid about the basic premise of the go go bars. I will get into some of the local and individual specifics later.

10. Peep Shows

Like go go bars, there are peep shows and then there are peep shows. The few peep shows that still exist in the United States mostly involve private booths divided by glass. A dancer strips on one side of the glass while a customer sits on the other, often masturbating themselves whether or not that is actually legal. As a general rule these places tend to be run down and staff uninspired women who have seen better days. They seem to be losing their appeal in the days of internet porn and travel. I don't how much longer the last of these places will hang on.

In Japan there is another type of peep show venue called a *nozokibeya* that is actually quite popular. In these peep shows there is one center stage that is surrounded by small private booths. Those in the booths can see out to the stage but not into the other booths.

Customers enter and pay an admission fee. When enough customers have gathered each man goes to his own booth. The booths are filled with chairs, garbage cans and tissues.

With the booths filled dancers come out and work the stage. Depending on the place there can be one or two dancers. They get fully nude and make sure to turn so that everyone in the booths can see every inch of them. Surprisingly the women tend to be incredibly good looking and fit gals in their twenties with bodies that look like they came out of a local version of Playboy magazine.

While some spendthrift customers masturbate themselves in the booths then leave, others flip a light switch that indicates a desire for extra services.

After the show is finished, the dancers come around to

each booth and provide the desired services. Vaginal intercourse is not offered as it is illegal, but hand jobs and blow jobs are usually on the menu. Other common options include touching a dancer above the waist or purchasing a dancer's panties.

The service is fast and furious with each customer given only a few minutes in a cramped booth, but the dancers tend to be experts at their work. Most customers leave satisfied.

Admission prices in these peep shows are usually around 2000 Yen ($18 USD) with additional services going for 1000 to 2000 Yen more.

New Hot Point in the Kabukicho section of Tokyo is one of the most famous nozokibeya peep shows in Japan. Madonna in the same area is another.

11. Short Time Bars

Short time bars are a lot like hostess bars except that they make sexual services more quickly and easily available. In short time bars the aim is to get customers to spend some money to have sex with one of the women on staff rather than to try to make money by extracting lady drinks.

The most famous strip of short time bars anywhere in the world is located on Soi 6 in Pattaya. This street is lined with bars on both sides for its duration. Hundreds of scantly clad women working the bars sit or stand in front of their venues doing everything they can to get customers inside. Inside the bars sex is sold in private rooms for 1000 Baht ($31 USD).

Cambodia is home to one or two hostess bars that could be called short time bars too. They aim more for getting customers to pay bar fines than buy drinks. Rooms in nearby hotels are used now that most places no longer all for sex on premises.

There are also short time bars in Nicaragua including the well known Fenix in Managua. In these bars women of typically average looks in their twenties hang around drinking with guys until a customer decides to take them into private room for a short round of sex. The price is typically around 600 Cordobas ($19 USD).

The famous Hooker Hill in Seoul, South Korea, could also be described as a place filled with short time bars. The thirty and forty year old women who work the many bars on "the hill" peer through the windows until they see a likely customer. Then they unlock their doors and come outside in an effort to attract the guy inside.

The bars on Hooker Hill are small and guys often find

that they are the only customer in the bar. They are typically offered a short round of sex either in the bar or in a nearby hotel room. Prices are typically around 70,000 Won ($62 USD) but some neophytes have reportedly been charged as much as 200,000.

12. Escorts and Independents

Escorts are women who meet men in exchange for payment. Some claim to "escort" guys in need of arm candy to events while others are more open and more or less admit that they sell sex.

Technically it could be said at least some escorts participate in compensated dating. Indeed that is the argument many escorts make in order to ply their trade openly. According to those escorts, customers pay them for their time and company. Anything else that happens is voluntary fun between consenting adults.

Some escorts work for agencies. Others work on their own. Those who work on their own are called independents.

There are also independent sex workers who put on no pretense of selling but sex. They could simply be referred to independents or perhaps independent sex workers.

Independents can work out of apartments or hotel rooms or simply use the internet to find customers.

In places like Hong Kong hundreds of independents work out of small apartments. In Saigon some independents ride around on motorbikes looking for lonely guys on the streets. All throughout the world elsewhere others use dating apps and "find people around me" features on chat apps to find horny guys nearby. Prices can vary greatly from one person and place to the next.

Today escorts and independents are quite common. Probably the biggest reason for that is the rise of the internet and to a certain extent the smart phone. With a worldwide communication network in the palm of nearly every hand, people are now free to interface in a way that they weren't just a few years ago.

13. Street Walkers

Street walkers are women who work streets in towns and cities looking for customers. Some service guys right in the streets while others do their work in vehicles or nearby rooms instead.

Street walkers are the stereotypes usually refereed to when people talk about prostitution. The popular narrative is that they are destitute and desperate and subject to abuse by basically everyone they come in contact with.

In reality street walkers come in all forms. Those in the United States or maybe Germany may tend more to be downtrodden. At the same time there are actually university students and other women with relatively stable lives who sometimes work famous strolls such as Beach Road in Pattaya.

Street walkers do tend to ask for the smallest amounts of any sex workers no matter where they are. In some places they work for as little as $10 US dollars. Then again, there are women in brothels around the work getting less than that for sex and splitting it with their managers.

There was a time in recent history when street walkers probably challenged compensated dating practitioners in terms of absolute numbers. I think that time has passed. Thanks to the internet and the proliferation of commercial sex venues of all sorts street walkers are not as common today as they once were. Don't be confused though. There are still many women walking streets around the world.

14. Scams, Sicknesses and Other Dangers

No report of the global commercial sex industry would be complete with at least a brief discussion on the various scams and dangers that exist.

In a general and overall sense I don't know that rip-offs are any more common in and around the sex industry than anywhere else once all in considered. Do guys get ripped off trying to pick up hookers in high crime areas? Absolutely. People in the same areas who aren't looking to purchase sex also run into crime on a regular basis.

Japan has a massive sex industry that may be among the largest and most lucrative in the world. The same country also has an incredibly low crime rate. At the same time the United States has a high rate of crime in relation to other "rich countries" yet prostitution is illegal in most of the country.

The most common complaints heard around the sex industry are things like "bait and switch" with providers using fake pictures or false promises to lure in customers, pick pocketing of guys chatting with street walkers or engaged in sex in brothels, and price inflation sometimes backed up by big muscular guys.

Yet at the same time there are countless sex workers and customers who participate in the industry regularly for decades without issue.

So why does sex work seem to have more criminal activity attached to it? Maybe it's because the scene is underground and illegal in many places allowing for anti-social activity to flourish. Maybe it's because participants are often too embarrassed or incriminated by their own actions to run to the authorities if they have a problem. I don't have a definitive answer, and I'm not even sure it's true that sex work and crime go hand and hand. There are too many examples of sex work around the world without such issues to ignore.

There are numerous reports from all around the world that sex workers are among the most at risk for carrying HIV. This too may go deeper than some would think.

I am not a scientist but I do read a lot of the reports on the questions. Many times it turns out that the sex workers who are most likely to have HIV are also on the low end of society. They may have been through harsh lives, abused, addicted to drugs, and regularly engaging in unprotected sex. Some studies suggest sex workers who earn less per session are more likely to get HIV while others claim the opposite. There is probably some correlation. High end escorts probably don't acquire

At the same time there are sex workers around the world who are regularly educated and tested. They tend to be among some of the least likely to acquire HIV and other sexually transmitted infections.

There are also sex workers who put in decades at blow job bars where they regularly give unprotected oral sex to several men per day yet retire without any obvious negative health effects.

The highest levels of HIV in the world are found in Swaziland. Prostitution is illegal there. In nearby Lesotho, prostitution is legal but HIV rates also high. One estimate says that more than 70 percent of sex workers in Lesotho are infected with HIV.

But we can again look at Japan. One of the largest sex industries in the world with millions of people involved, yet Japan has one of the lowest rates of HIV infection in the world. The same goes for South Korea where prostitution is common but HIV infections are rare. Clearly sex work isn't the only thing at play.

That fact is that most sex workers do not acquire HIV even if some do. The same goes for most customers of sex workers. This is not to discount the risks at all. The risk of HIV very certainly exists for sex workers and their clients.

There is also risk for all sorts of other sexually transmitted diseases and things like pregnancy for the people involved. Not all of this risk can be mitigated by the use of condoms either.

The risk exists for people who don't exchange money for sex too. Homosexuals and drug users are typically the most at risk, but heterosexual sex can absolutely spread the virus too. In some places prostitutes are regularly tested for disease and use condoms for everything. Can that be said of all the people who have sex without payment?

Risk can never be totally eliminated from life. People regularly die in automobile accidents yet billions continue to use vehicles every day.

Ultimately people weigh the risks of any activity they undertake against the rewards and then make the best go at it they can. That applies as much to the commercial sex industry as anything else in life.

III. Shopping For It

Now that you know the ins and outs of the pay for play game, you may be curious as to how customers and clients find each other. In same cases such as red light districts it is rather obvious. Other cases, such as independents who use smartphone applications, have already been described. What about the rest?

There was a time when taxi drivers were the number one source of information for a new arrival in any city in the world. When a stranger showed up in a strange land, they typically hoped in a cab. On their way to their quarters or wherever else they were heading, it was common for these travelers to ask the cabbie about prostitutes. Often, they didn't even have to ask. The drivers would bring up the subject with single men on their own. And as experienced guys on the ground, they knew what they were talking about and where they were headed.

This is perfectly illustrated by the example of a guy who went from taxi driver to prominent adult writer. Previously a New York City cab driver, the guy knew where a lot the local sex work went on. When customers asked about prostitution, he took them to places where it was available.

He knew about the Korean massage parlors, the Chinese massage parlors, the streetwalkers, the peep shows and even a lot of under the radar brothels. He saw the comings and goings around them too. With that knowledge base he was well suited to move into marketing for the adult industry. He went on to manage the escort ads section of a popular newspaper before getting into making and selling ads himself. Later he started writing on his own and publishing a lot of information and anecdotes.

Guys looking for sex aren't as likely to ask taxi drivers today as they were years ago, but it still happens. In some places it's still pretty common. For example visitors of countries like Cambodia often end up in brothels they could never find on their own by asking taxi drivers to take them somewhere for a sexual massage. Even in growing and modern China it is common for guys to ask cab drivers about prostitution since censorship and crackdowns there are so common that they force much of the adult activity into the underground.

In some places like Bangkok, there are drivers who try to force things on guys too. That's usually because they get paid a commission for taking a guy to a place. Big soapy massage parlors in particular seem to reward drivers for bringing in customers.

After taxi drivers, trade publications were once among the most common place for guys seeking to buy sex to find providers at least in certain parts of the world. In other parts of the world however, such things have never really existed.

This seems to depend more on social standards than the laws on the books or even the actual reality. For example there are countries with huge commercial sex industries that operate more or less in the open like Thailand, the Dominican Republic or the Philippines where such publications would be absolutely unthinkable. Yet in the United States where sex work is mostly illegal and underground there are things like newspapers dedicated to strip clubs or even massage!

There don't seem to be many sex trade publications around anymore. Most written information has moved to the internet as I will soon explain. There are still some publications around however.

In Japan there are actually several publications dedicated in full or in part to the massive local sex industry. They are published regularly and sold openly. There is even one publication made up mainly of job listings for such work that women can peruse!

Manzoku and *Naitai* are probably the best known of these kinds of publications in Japan. They are widely read though more people probably rely on the internet now to find such information, even in Japan where the sex industry is huge and magazines are still somewhat popular.

Unsurprisingly, some Japanese language magazines covering the sex industries in other countries have appeared too. For example there is a Japanese magazine published in Thailand with information on the many sex shops there. Perhaps because it is written in Japanese, it doesn't seem to be targeted by the powers that be.

In places like the United States where specific sex industry publications rarely exist, alternative newspapers became a popular place for sex workers to advertise.

Papers like the Village Voice in New York City had back pages full of thinly-veiled ads for prostitution in the form of "body work," "massage" or "escorts." There were also the text ads and the personals.

In fact, the infamous "Backpage" website recently shut down by the government for prostitution related issues was so named because of this old practice. Everyone knew the "back page" of the Village Voice and papers like it was a place where prostitutes advertised their services not so long ago.

The ads weren't reviewed and usually included no real information. Instead there would usually be a photo of some anonymous model, one or two words, and a phone number or address. Some escorts were bold enough to show at least partial pictures of themselves, but they were in the minority.

The practice of advertising sex work in alternative newspapers in the US was once so well known that law enforcement sometimes even went as far as running phony ads in these publications. When customers showed up for service they were arrested and often publicly shamed.

For visitors and even long-term residents looking to purchase sexual service these alternative papers were once a major source of information. Today such a thing barely exists. They were never shut down. Instead changes in society simply moved things along.

In the summer of 2012, Village Voice publicly disowning one of its corporate advertising partners that ran ads for a wide variety of adult services. Backpage then became a major website before coming under fire and eventually being shutdown. The same information and ads are still around, but now they are a little more scattered around.

Without a doubt, the internet has changed pretty much everything when it comes to commercial sex industry information. In some cases it even changed the industry itself.

There are literally thousands, maybe even tens of thousands, of websites, blogs and discussion forums organized around discussion of the sex trade. I'm not even talking about pornography here, although there is even more of that now too than there used to be, including a fair share themed or based on the idea of the skin trade. I'm talking about websites that concentrate on people and places involved in pay for play sexual activities.

When I first started writing about the commercial sex industry years ago there weren't many sites in the niche. Now there are countless. Personal websites recounting the tales of customers seem to be growing fastest, while collaborative discussion forum and review efforts appear to be somewhat in decline.

In the case of many review type sites, writers by and large have no motivation to be dishonest. They aren't running businesses, so they have no reason to show fake pictures, concoct positive reviews or lie about services. Those who do tell tall tales for whatever reason are often called out by others if the discussion is open. Countless sex shop shills have tried to post positive reviews of their own businesses on websites like the gigantic "International Sex Guide" only to be torn apart by other contributors.

On top of the review and informational websites, there are numerous sites with classified ads. These sites which operate to some degree like the back pages of alternative newspapers described above.

Some of these sites allow service providers to post freely. Some charge the providers to post. Some take commissions of various types. Most of these rely on returning visitors. No provider would want to pay them for listing if they didn't have an audience. But things are changing in this area too, and classified sites are either disappearing or blocking any talk of sex or even dating more and more.

Craigslist was probably the most infamous general site to have hosted adult listings. That is not longer the case. After a few mentally ill predators apparently sought out victims through this medium the erotic gigs section of the site was shut down under immense pressure. Of course none of this ended the trade or really even limited its promotion on Craigslist. Listings for adult services kept appearing in the "therapeutic services" section of the site, or in the "no strings attached" or "women for man" dating sections instead.

More recently even the dating sections have been removed from Craigslist, apparently out of fear of recent legal actions and crackdowns.

Advertisements aren't as common as they used to be in any event. It used to be common to see adverts for all sorts of sex services posted on websites that discuss the issue. Nowadays it is not so common. Social developments probably explain that too.

The information is still there though in some form of another. In some cases it might not even be recognizable. For example, there are many women around the world posting profiles on dating websites in order to find paying customers. It's just another form of the same thing.

Finally there are the websites run by people in the commercial sex industry themselves. Examples of this are websites for erotic massage parlors or go go bars. Escorts and independents often maintain websites too. Sometimes they do it under the cover of "modeling" complete with "portfolios" filled with their photographs.

Increasingly adult entertainment and sex work providers are forgoing websites altogether however and simply setting up pages or accounts for themselves on social media platforms like Twitter and Facebook instead. Many large businesses officially prohibit anything to do with sex work but in practice these accounts are commonly tolerated or at least ignored. Only time will tell how long this will last.

IV. Searching For It

Above I gave a fairly detailed explanation of the various types of sex workers and the venues they typically work out of. By and large these generalities apply around the world.

Of course there are local variations and things can look different from one place to the next. For example, blow job bars in Japan and Thailand both provide a similar service but they do so in a different way.

Next I will give basic rundowns on the commercial sex scenes as they exist in a variety of countries all around the world. I think you'll see that there is a lot of variation around the globe and one constant: guys are paying for sex, and women are selling it.

1. The United States

The United States is commonly referred to as "the freest country in the world." The validity of that is true is not something for this book to debate. But you have to wonder about such a claim when prostitution is illegal everywhere but a few small brothels outside of Las Vegas.

Regardless of the laws on the books, the commercial sex scene is actually quite large in the United States, even in places you probably would never expect. The industry varies a lot by region. There are places where it's pretty much out in the open and tolerated and there are places where providers are hounded to the point that they are driven underground. In that way, it somewhat like marijuana which can be smoked openly in one city and summarily banned in another.

Across the board those who dare to participate in the consensual exchange of sexual services for money in America typically practice quite a bit or discretion. Even where the industry is seemingly more accepted, it still operates on a more or less underground level.

A wide range of individuals and venues offer sexual services in the United States. Everything from the well-known massage parlors and street walkers to strip clubs that offer certain extras and cafes staffed by big breasted babes who are known to give customers a wank for a tip exist. The following is a brief run down of some of the most common types of sex work in America.

Streetwalkers ply their trade in many major cities and even in some more rural areas too despite the existence and widespread adoption of the internet. Women who work the streets of the US in this day and age are often in a sorry state and clearly need help. Those who pick up or are even suspected of cruising for streetwalkers are exposed to threats of arrest, disease, robbery and general unpleasantness.

Further, streetwalkers are not known for offering great services by even their most regular customers. Not much can be expected from women who are often desperate and drug addicted and forced to work in the confined quarters of cars while under the constant threat of arrest.

Strip clubs are common in most of the United States. Although they seemingly banned from some of the most conservative parts of the country, you can even find them in rural areas.

Strip clubs vary widely in quality and regulation. This is another feature of the United States and its unique regional form of social organization. Three clubs in the same state may be entirely different, depending on local laws. One may be have fully nude dancers on stage while dancers in another may only be topless. A third club may be staffed by women who wear bikinis full time. Despite the various laws, there are women working strip clubs who offer sexual services to paying customers willing to shell out bigger than average tips.

What is permitted in strip clubs seems to be largely decided by local management and culture. In some places customers suckle the breasts of dancers right out in the open while others have their penises rubbed through their pants in semi-private lap dance areas. In others blow jobs are commonly performed in VIP rooms. In still other strip clubs customers are not allowed to come anywhere near dancers with so called "air dances" being sold to guys who want to watch a lady dance in front of them for extra money.

Most strip clubs in the US today are probably totally legal, especially as the corporate model becomes more common. Rules can be strict. Clubs don't want to risk being shut down because one girl wants to make more money on the side, especially when the clubs don't even get a piece of the action.

Escort agencies proliferate through urban area across the United States. They used to advertise in phone books when those were common. Nowadays they seem to use the internet to find customers in most cases.

Officially, these places are staffed with women available only for companionship. Whatever else happens is between the consenting adults involved and has nothing to do with payment. In practice "whatever else happens" is usually sex. It usually has a pretty specific price attached to it too.

There are also independent escorts operating all over the country. Many even travel or "tour" regularly. The independents may get less customers but charge more. That's not always the case however.

Prices charged by escorts in the US can vary greatly. Some ask for as little as $160 to meet a guy for a short rendezvous. So-called high class escorts can charge thousands as the case of "anti-prostitution" New York politician Eliot Spitzer proved. Most escorts charge something in between. Recently it seems that agency women are commonly starting with quotes of $300 while independents lean more towards $800 as a starting fee.

Compensated dating may now be outpacing formal escorting in the US. Websites like Seeking Arrangement are exploding in popularity and even some regular dating websites and applications are filled with women who announce a desire to be paid for their time by sugar daddies either directly or indirectly.

Acceptance and even expectation of pay for play seems to be spreading throughout American society. In her chart topping song "Bodak Yellow" former stripper turned best selling musician boats:

I might just feel on your babe

My pussy feel like a lake
He wanna swim with his face
I'm like okay
I'll let him do what he want
He buy me Yves Saint Laurent

She proudly proclaims that she will engage in sexual activity with attached men as long as they buy her expensive apparel, and she becomes a star in the process.

This seems like one of many indications that the sale of sexual services for cash isn't something that everyone or even most people in America are against, despite what the laws may state.

And what about Nevada, where prostitution is actually legal and regulated in some areas? Sex work abounds across the state. It might even be more common in Las Vegas, where it is actually illegal, than in the counties with legal brothels

The regulated brothels are few and far between. They're also far from the bright lights of Las Vegas that draw most people to the state.

Prices are not publicly advertised, apparently due to local regulations, but they tend to be much higher than those of the many brothels and erotic massage parlors in Vegas. In some cases the brothels charge much more than even escorts who work the casinos and areas around them.

The women in the legal brothels range in looks but as far as I know no one considers them rivals for top models. They render all sexual services with condoms with compares with black market sex workers in the state who often do oral and always do hand jobs without the use of a rubber.

The legal brothels remain somewhat popular but for the above reasons and more they certainly haven't driven the many unofficial sex workers in the state out of business. Under the current model it seems highly unlikely they ever will.

That brings me to the next type of commercial sex venue, which is perhaps the most well known of all: the massage parlor.

I have described erotic massage earlier. I go much further in breaking down each type of erotic massage parlor that exists in my book "Happy Ending Massage: The Complete Report."

Generally speaking there are a few types of erotic massage venue in the US. There are Chinese massage parlors, Korean massage parlors, Russian massage parlors, Thai massage parlors and American massage parlors.

On top of that there are individual and independent massage providers as well as tantric massage practitioners.

Legitimate massage parlors can be eliminated from the discussion since they do not offer erotic services as a general rule. These can range from the corporate-owned fake spa chains like "Massage Envy" where erotic services absolutely are not available to locally owned Chinese or American shops where masseuses sometimes "accidentally" bump into the genitals of customers in hopes of leading them on so they pay for more massage time. The subject at hand here is erotic massage which is offered at different sorts of shops.

When one thinks of an Asian massage parlor that offers happy endings, their mind most likely conjures up images of Chinese massage parlors, even if they don't know it. Undoubtedly the most common type of massage shop in the United States, Chinese massage parlors exist in every major city and a huge number of suburban and even rural areas.

Massage has been around in China for thousands of years. The *Huangdi Nei-jing*, which is considered the foundation of traditional Chinese medicine, was created sometime between 475 - 220 BC. It contains no less than 30 references to massage. The practice of massage has continued on ever since then in China, even through all of the country's tumultuous history. With the seemingly endless opportunity to make money doing rub downs that exists in the United States, the ancient practice of Chinese massage has been updated, imported and applied widely; a lot like General Tso's Chicken.

When I say Chinese massage parlor I am talking about a particular kind of place. I am not describing every massage parlor with a Chinese name or Chinese people on staff. Obviously there are massage parlors with Chinese names, staff or owners that do not offer anything other than regular old body rubs. On the other hand there are some Chinese owned and staffed places that offer more than just mainstream massages to customers. Those places which have come to be known as "Chinese massage parlors" in circles with an interest in Asian massage parlors are the places I am now describing.

Chinese massage parlors can be found all over the United States. They often provide body massages along with additional erotic services.

Usually single male customers who visit a Chinese massage parlor will get a poor to decent massage followed by a hand job hand ending finish. On some occasions, especially in "fly by night" setups in residential buildings that come and go from one day to the next, customers may be offered oral sex or even full service.

There are various hints and signs that can help customers figure out whether or not a Chinese massage parlor offers sexual services. If it is open into the late night or early morning or advertises on websites with adult or personal classified ad sections there's a good chance there are extras on offer.

Where extras are on offer at a Chinese massage parlor it's accepted as a normal part of the massage. The logic is that such activity is necessary for "full release" on the part of the male clientele. At least that's the theory. In some cases the simple fact is that masseuses massage particular body parts so that they can make more money in the form of tips than their often meager standard salaries provide otherwise.

Chinese massage parlors often operate in a sort of gray area and service follows as such. These aren't usually straight forward brothels where guys just walk in and get wanked off. Instead they are places where massages are concluded with offers for further work on the parts between the thighs.

This is by design and intended both for the safety of the staff and venues and as a part of creating an overall relaxing atmosphere. After all relaxation is the entire point of massage.

If extras are on offer masseuses will normally make it known. They don't typically wait for customers to make a move. Any guy who shows up at a massage parlor being aggressive and pushing for more than a massage would be asking for trouble. In fact such behavior would probably be illegal and grounds for a masseuse to end a session or even call in law enforcement.

Frequent visitors to happy ending massage parlors in the United States don't normally ask for any extra services. They simply lay back and receive them as they come. Some masseuses who do offer extra services may even turn down a guy who asks for them directly since they could fear that the customer is in fact a member of some law enforcement agency trying to cause a problem. The law is often among the biggest fears of sex workers in the United States and many other parts of the world for reasons that should be obvious.

Nowadays the internet offers a wide range of information that was not available to massage parlor aficionados even a few years ago. While some guys will still "take one for the team" and visit a massage parlor not covered online to see if they can get a happy ending, the vast majority of customers today research massage parlors in advance in order to find a place to their liking. That has become slightly more difficult with recent laws that have restricted sex related speech on the internet but things are still discussed online rather openly often on websites hosted in countries with speech protections still intact.

When a guy looking for a happy ending enters a massage parlor for the first time they typically ask for a one hour massage. That's true even when a 30 minute massage is available for less money. That is because as a first time visitor they are more likely to get extras with a one hour massage than they are with twenty or thirty minute sessions. Guys who opt for a short session may be branded as a "cheap charlie" off the bat and receive nothing more than a mediocre rub down.

Unlike staff at some Korean massage parlors the women who work at Chinese massage parlors in the United States almost never wear any kind of sexy lingerie. While some of the higher end and better established places may have Chinese women in their twenties in somewhat sexy uniforms on staff the vast majority of Chinese massage parlors have middle aged or even older women working. Of course looks are no indication of skill and some of the oldest women are the most renown for their abilities.

The staff at most Chinese massage parlors will ask unfamiliar customers if they have visited before. Some sources say that guys who want extra service must answer yes to this question no matter what the truth actually is. I don't believe that is true. Guys who say things like "no, but I go to another place" or "no, but my friend told me to come here" seem just as likely to get extra services. Even those who truthfully say "no" and leave it at that are often offered extras.

The usual rate at Chinese massage parlors is 40 to 50 US dollars for an hour massage. Some places may ask for as much as 80 or even 100. There are also some cheaper places around but they are becoming rarer with each passing day. Payment is typically rendered after a massage is given though some places may ask for payment up front if they feel there is a risk of being shorted.

The most high end Chinese massage parlors offer table showers. These involve the customer laying down on a padded table in a wash room and being cleaned from head to toe. Some middle of the road places will allow customers to shower themselves in a private stand up shower before or after the massage. Most places will offer no kind of showering whatsoever.

At the start of massage sessions customers are led to a room and told to take off their clothes. Some rooms are plain but normal with walls that go up to the ceiling and locking doors. Other rooms are made up of nothing more than some thin dividers arranged around a massage table with a curtain for a door.

For an oil massage in a Chinese massage parlor it is normal for the customer to get naked. Some customers who were fearful or nervous and left their underwear on have been told to remove them even at so called legitimate massage places. That's because it is difficult to do an oil massage on a customer wearing underwear.

Most regulars at happy ending massage parlors say they get naked and sit down waiting for their masseuse to return though others report covering themselves up with a towel. The idea some have is that customers who show they are comfortable in the nude put the masseuses at ease and lessen any idea that the customers may in fact be cops.

In any event after the masseuse enters the room the customer is told to lay down face first on the table. Their body is then covered up in a towel. The towel is moved around as the massage progresses but is normally not totally removed from the body until much later.

As mentioned, massages at Chinese massage parlors are typically done with the use of oil. Some customers don't want to be covered in oil. They have different reasons for this. Some don't want to be oiled up if they can't shower afterwards. Some fear that suspicious significant others will notice the oil on their bodies. Some simply find it uncomfortable. Normally customers can request that a massage be done without oil but in that case it is a lot less comfortable. In some cases a sort of talcum powder can be used instead of oil.

With or without oil the masseuses often ask customers if they want a hard or soft massage with their limited English. A hard massage involves varying amounts of pressure being applied to the back, buttocks and legs. A soft massage usually means the masseuse will lightly run her fingers over the body, giving the customer goosebumps and quite possibly getting him erect. Customers focused on getting a happy ending will usually ask for a soft massage if given the option. The idea behind that is that soft massage is more likely to lead to a happy ending. That's why people on websites about massage parlors often refer to a happy ending as "soft touch" when they write reviews.

Some who frequent Chinese massage parlors report that they will try to touch their masseuses lightly on the leg during their massages. According to them the masseuses will pull away if extras are not available or stay put if they are. I don't think there's much validity to this. In any case it sounds quite creepy.

I have no way to know for sure but I would imagine that most masseuses would much prefer that customers simply try to strike up a conversation with them. They would probably appreciate it and even be happy to be able to practice their English and get a break from the monotony of rubbing the backs of semi-sleeping guys day after day.

During the massage things will often get a bit sexy at least from the point of view of the customer. When the masseuse is rubbing legs, buttocks and thighs customers often get turned on. This doesn't seem to be much of a problem even for places that don't offer extras.

Since erections can be totally involuntary during a massage they are often ignored. On the other hand customers who maintain an erection for a sustained period of time are probably more likely to be noticed.

At some point during any massage customers are asked to flip over and lie on their back. That's where things can get iffy though it all becomes clear soon enough.

So, after getting their legs and backsides rubbed customers will sometimes be erect. Flipping over and having the towel moved makes that very obvious. Sometimes a masseuse will ask the question "do you want to turn over?" For guys in the know that itself can be an offer for extras. More usually the masseuse just says "turn over" or "flip" and starts rubbing the inside of the legs. Eventually, if extras are offered, the masseuse will move closer to the penis and balls. They may even tease the groin or go as far as grabbing the stick or nuts. At that point they will either move directly to performing a hand job or they will ask the customer questions like "do you want anything else?," or make a hand motion signaling a hand job and ask "okay?"

At most Chinese massage places in America where extras are on offer prices are not discussed before hand. When prices are discussed up front it is often a sign of poor services to come although there are exception. In any case, hand job happy endings can range from fast and mechanical to slow, oily and erotic. No matter the style of service customers nearly always get emptied out sooner rather than later.

During a happy ending at a Chinese massage parlor the masseuse may get topless or even naked but this is usually not the case. Some regulars find that they can gain more access to their masseuses if they visit repeatedly and offer to tip more once the service is already underway.

Most masseuses do seem to be okay with customers touching them over their clothes during a happy ending hand job but some are not. Since it's all a gray area there are no hard and fast rules. Ultimately the easiest way for anyone to get consent is usually to ask for it but human interactions can be complicated.

At the completion of a happy ending customers are usually cleaned up by the masseuse with either tissues or warm wet towels. After that the masseuse leaves the room. Customers them get dressed and head out to the front desk to pay. At around the same time customer give their masseuses a tip directly for their services. In a few cases when the owners of a place are unaware of extra services being offered, or at least pretend to be unaware, masseuses sometimes request that their tips be given discreetly in the privacy of the room.

There aren't any hard and fast rules but generally speaking the normal tip for a hand job at a Chinese massage parlor in the United States is around forty dollars. Obviously some guys give more. A few may even give less but they are less likely to receive good or even any service if they return. At times masseuses will come right out and ask for a certain amount and it is sometimes more than forty dollars.

Again, not every Chinese masseuse does happy endings! If at the end of a massage the masseuse simply says "okay that's it" and leaves the room, that means extras aren't being offered. Guys who explore massage parlors in an attempt to find places that offer happy ending accept that possibility. That's part of their fun. The standard tip at places that do not offer happy endings is around ten dollars.

After a customer becomes familiar with a Chinese massage place that offers extra services they often return. Once they are known they are more likely to get the services they are looking for with far less uncertainty. They may may opt for a 30 minute massage if the happy ending is all they're after. In that case the tip remains the same. They may also inquire about four and even six handed massages which ads another masseuse or two to the mix. That is available at many Chinese massage parlors that offer extras and even some that don't. Obviously each masseuse involved expects to be tipped for any many handed massage.

Earlier I alluded to fly by night Chinese massage places set up in houses and apartments. In the past these less common set ups could be found in listings in the backs of alternative papers. Later the ads migrated to the internet. They are usually short and to the point, saying things like "Asian massage, 555-555-5555."

Since these places are private and often located in residential areas where business is not technically allowed customers have to call ahead to make an appointment and get directions. These spots are discreet. Customers sometimes have to call two or even three times to gain admission. Then they are let inside only to have one or two doors locked behind them.

Once inside, customers typical receive a half-assed massage and then are asked what else they want. Hand jobs are standard services offered in these kinds of places but sometimes customers will be offered oral sex.

Some of the women will perform oral sex without protection, especially if they're older, but others require it even if its not effective. Customers who don't bring their own condoms will sometimes find masseuses in these places doing something strange like covering the penis in plastic wrap before popping it in their mouth.

Guys who become regular and trusted visitors of these places can be offered full service by women who get to know them or take a liking to them. The women who perform full service obviously do it because they can get more money but there are cases when they simply want to get some enjoyment for themselves and take the opportunity of using a trusted guy to get off on.

In these places prices will normally be negotiated up front. Customers may pay 40 dollars for an hour massage then negotiate other costs for further services. Sometimes customers can get away with paying a lot less than they would pay at a "normal" Chinese jack shack like those described above.

I am aware of at least one place were the sexy middle-aged Chinese manager also did massages herself. She got really into her work and went above and beyond the call of duty. She'd jerk and blow customers with her big boobs out without even asking for a tip! At forty dollars a go all included it was quite a bargain in comparison to the competition. Of course it didn't last. These places never last. That's something regular customers are aware of.

As you should be able to tell from reading this, things are widely variable with Chinese massage parlors. Fans of the places usually have laid back attitudes and simply go with whatever comes.

Korean massage parlors differ from the Chinese variety of massage parlors in several ways. The main thing that sets them apart is the type of services offered. With few exceptions, Korean massage parlors offer full service, which of course is a euphemism for intercourse.

A table shower, which involves the customer laying on a covered massage table while being soaped up and rinsed by a masseuse, is also standard. That's a bonus both for the client and the woman servicing him who doesn't have to deal with any unnecessary body odors.

How can you tell if a massage parlor is Chinese or Korean? For those who know the difference between the Chinese and Korean people and their languages this is very easy. For others there are a number of clues that stand out.

Do customers have to call the place to find out the location? There's a good chance it's Korean. Is it open 24 hours or at least very late? There's a good chance it's Korean. Does the massage parlor or "spa" have a website with pictures of the girls who work there scantly clad in modeling poses? Then it's most likely Korean. Does it have all of the features above? Then it's most likely a Korean place. Online scouting can also indicate which places are Korean rather than Chinese. There are now numerous sites where people share information on Asian massage parlors in the US on a regular basis.

How do people find Korean massage parlors? There was a time when potential customers were limited to word of mouth and looking around town unless they could get their hands on alternative newspapers. The Yellow Pages were even an option back then. Some places had big ads placed under "massage." Today guys looking for Korean massage parlors typically seek out specific massage review websites out there like Rub Maps.

Obviously when I talk about "Korean massage parlors" I am not saying every massage parlor owned or staffed by Koreans operates in this way. That is definitely not the case. I am simply describing a particular category of adult oriented massage parlor that exists in the United States.

Korean massage parlors exist in most major cities and to a much lesser extent in some small towns. The prices and services are pretty much standard. In New York and other large cities customers typically pay $200 US dollars all in. In some smaller cities they'll pay 160 or 180. Guys who act like they don't know whats going on may be asked for a lot more. It's pretty rare for a customer to be ripped off in a Korean massage parlor even if they are a complete newbie but it does happen. Customers who are knowledgeable and prepared typically don't deal with that issue at all.

When guys visit a Korean massage parlor for the first time they usually call ahead to make an appointment or at least see if there is any availability. With a lot of places that is a necessity since the massage parlors don't list their exact locations in ads or on websites.

Customers usually need to call from an unblocked number. A lot of Korean massage parlors won't answer phone calls from private numbers. In the US cheap prepaid phones are easy to get and guys with discretion issues usually come up with a fake name. Nowadays there are even apps that let people temporarily use a phone number then discard it. So there are a lot of guys with names like "Joe" and "Frank" calling from burner phones and numbers that disappear from one day to the next.

In select big cities like New York a lot of Korean massage parlors have websites that feature pictures of the women on staff. When guys find a particular woman on a parlor's website attractive they can ask to set an appointment with her. In smaller cities that's a lot less common. Even where websites are available they don't always reflect reality.

In any event customers usually call ahead before visiting a Korean massage parlor. If they are regular visitors or the place has a more stable and well advertised location customers also have the option of just dropping in unannounced though they then run the risk of being turned away at the door.

When customers arrive at a Korean massage parlor they usually need to ring a doorbell. Most Korean massage parlors have secure steel doors with several locks in front. They also tend to have video cameras above the door so they can see who is outside before they open their doors. This is meant to keep out unwanted "surprise visitors" like robbers or other more devious creatures from simply stopping by. Customers typically arrive alone and are able to gain entrance by smiling at the camera and waiting.

New customers at any Korean massage parlor are usually asked if they have been there before. Lying in these places often doesn't work because unlike the massage girls the managers, often called mamasans, tend to stick around for a while and have good memories. In some cases they even keep record books with names and numbers of customers that they share with other managers to block out undesirable customers. Educated guys who want to enter a Korean massage parlor for the first time usually say that they have been to other parlors before and have decided to try a new location. Or they simply say that a friend recommended the place. Of course guys aren't necessarily turned away if they just say "no, I haven't." It depends on the situation.

After gaining entrance to a Korean massage parlor customers are led into a private room. Sometimes the manager will do the leading. At other times a masseuse will. The masseuses in the Korean massage parlors are most often more attractive than those at the Chinese parlors. They are usually dressed in a revealing nightie or other sexy garb too.

The Korean women who work in the Korean massage parlors usually come to the United States as visitors or live there permanently and rotate around any number of parlors. They normally don't stay in any one place too long though some do maintain permanent homes.

In the bigger cities, they staff at Korean massage parlors are typically made up of very attractive women in their twenties and thirties. Quite often they have well shaped large fake breasts and nice hair and makeup. In the smaller cities the women working the Korean massage parlors will usually be less attractive and often older gals that have aged out of the big city scene. They are still attractive enough in most cases and are commonly very skilled at their jobs. At one time these were the hotties in their twenties working in New York and Los Angeles. In some rare cases especially in more rural areas some of the women working in Korean massage parlors are at the end of middle age or older. Surprisingly they still do get customers. If they didn't they wouldn't be in the game.

Customers usually pay either the mamasan upon entry or the massage gal as soon as they get into the room. The standard rate is 60 per hour though it may be more in some places. Shops may offer a half hour session or they may not but guys in the know always opt for the hour to show that they're serious. They are also prepared and pay in cash. This money goes to the house.

Customers also have to pay for the extras. In New York and perhaps some other of the biggest cities the standard rate for full service is between 140 and 160 dollars and has been that way for some time. In the rest of the United States it varies between 100 and 140 on top of the house fee. All together the rates for service at a Korean massage parlor in America range from $160 to 220 USD.

Either immediately after asking for the house payment or a few minutes into the pathetic excuse for a massage that's provided customers will usually be asked what they want. In some places the masseuses will offer first timers lesser action like a hand job or blow job. This seems to be a way of testing new customers out. On repeat visits the same customers are sometimes offered full service. More commonly though it is simply expected that customers are looking for full service and so they are charged accordingly with no questions asked.

Korean massage parlor regulars tend to simply hand over the total amount together with the house fee all at once to show that they know the deal and are ready for action. Guys who opt for a hand job or blow job have to negotiate their own rates. They won't pay more than the going rate for full service.

When customers make appointments with a specific girl then that girl tends to be the service provider they get. When guys don't request a particular woman they are given whoever is next in rotation. Some experienced customers will ask for a "lineup" of available women to choose from though this is considered bad form. It is a common practice in Korea but the Koreans working in the United States don't seem to like it much. There are reasons these women work in the US to begin with. Since they often refuse to service Korean customers all together it seems that one of their motivations may be to get away from particular types of customers.

Korean massage parlors are usually clean and neat. The rooms are always private with complete walls that go up to the ceiling and locking doors. Some of the parlors are subdivided with thin walls so customers can hear what's going on outside of their rooms to some small extent but guys won't run into any paper walls or curtain "doors" like they'll find in some Chinese parlors.

Upon entering a private room customers are told to take off their clothes and wait. Sometimes the masseuse will stay in the room to watch or help the customer get undressed. Other times they will leave for a few minutes. When the customer tenders payment the girl will leave the room to give it to the house mom. Sometimes this is all combined into one action when a masseuse says something like "please give me the money and get undressed." In any case the customers simply sit tight and wait for their service providers to return.

Some Korean massage parlors give customers clear plastic pouches for their phones and wallets. This is so those valuables can be carried into the table shower and sauna. That ensures that nothing is stolen and that no one can pretend anything was taken either.

After taking off their clothes customers are normally given a towel. Experienced guys sometimes make sure their masseuse sees them naked before wrapping the towel around their body if they are at a new place. This is intended to let the service provider know what she's working with and help relax her a little bit keeping in mind they have a large number of things to worry about from customers who just walk in off the street. The thinking is that if the guy is cool she will be more likely to be too.

After undressing, customers will either be offered a table shower or simply led to a wash room. They put on the provided slippers and follow their masseuses to be bathed. Korean massage parlors are great at discretion and organization. Although a guy might hear another customer enter he will probably never ever actually see one inside.

Once customers enter the shower room they disrobe and

wait for the masseuse to spray some warm water on a big table specially designed for table showers. If a customer lays on the table before it's prepared he'll not only look like a newbie he'll also run the risk of freezing his nuts off!

After the table has been cleaned and prepared customers are told to lay down face first on the table. This is typically the time the service providers feel out their customers. As they lather up the clients they may get into some small talk. The nicer the guys are during the table shower the better chance they have at getting superior service later.

After the service providers wash the customers from head to toe–including the butt hole–thoroughly, they say "turn over" and start to wash the front. Sometimes they will get playful when they wash the cock and balls but other times they will not. Guys who get hard at this point may give the kind of signal the masseuse is looking for but even those who stay limp are likely to get similar service since they've already gone far enough for most service providers to be comfortable. In addition, when experienced customers are offered mouthwash they take it. That may mean they're going to be allowed to kiss or do more later. Any customers who refuse mouthwash when offered run the risk of being refused themselves.

Once customer are washed and dried they are either led to a small sauna room or directly back to the private massage room. Sometimes the service providers ask if the customers want to use the sauna. If a Korean massage parlor is particularly busy sometimes they will put the customer in a steam room for storage while they do some work in another room. Customers who do end up in the sauna simply wait there until their masseuses return.

Back in the private rooms the customers are given a perfunctory massage. Experienced guys know not to expect any pain relief here at all. It's almost unheard of to get a decent massage in a Korean parlor. But that's not why guys visit them. Sometimes a customer will get nothing more than a few seconds of "soft massage" which involves the masseuse gently gliding her fingers on the customer's skin to get him relaxed and in the mood. Sometimes the service providers will do a few minutes of half-assed massage. And sometimes they'll get right to work with the sexual services.

If they didn't get their work supplies while the customer was in the sauna the masseuses will often leave at this point to retrieve them. They all have small bags containing lube and condoms that they use with their clients.

Once the massage ends and the supplies are retrieved customers are told to lie down on the massage table on their backs. A lot of times the more professional girls will already have filled their pussies with lubricant so as not to ruin the mood.

Customers may get a cat bath which involves being licked all over with a special concentration on the nipples and balls. Sometimes the anus is also orally stimulated. This is all popular and common in Asia. It appears in varying degrees in Korean massage parlors in America.

The service providers then get their customers hard and apply a condom usually by using their mouth. Most of the service providers at Korean massage parlors are very good at this. More than one man has expressed his amazement at their ability to get hard instantly in these situations when they previously suffered from what was labeled erectile dysfunction. Many have also voiced amazement over the ability of some Korean service providers to apply a condom by mouth in a way that left them wondering if a condom was ever put on at all.

Korean service providers working in massage parlors typically use Asian condoms that are very thin and very high quality. They apply these then perform oral sex for a varying amount of time. Some will suck their customer and work his nuts with their hands for quite a while. Some will only give a few mechanical up and down oral motions.

One woman who worked at a shop in the Midwest used to do her best to make customers blow their loads early on with her "magic mouth". Those are her words, not mine. She wasn't very attractive. She had an older worn face and big, badly installed bolt-on tits. I'm sure most of her customers did not mind finishing by fellatio. Experienced customers who come close to cumming with hotter girls early on when things are still in the oral stage would probably be more likely to ask to slow down so there would be an opportunity for vaginal intercourse if they were dealing with someone other than old magic mouth.

As the main event unfolds the masseuses climb on top of their customers and start riding. Customers who want to go down on a service provider have to ask for that before the bucking begins. I can't be sure but I would guess that most customers skip the cunnilingus and get right in the routine. That would explain why the service providers normally go from blowing to humping. One thing to note is that while requests for oral either way are usually accepted, vaginal fingering is normally not permitted.

Once the full service begins some providers will allow all kinds of roaming hands and kissing. Others are princess-like and want none of it. Some treat their tits like prize possessions and will shy away from even nipple licking by customers. Others will let the customer have at it. Guys in the know just go with the flow, as they even tend to find their "bad" experiences in these places quite enjoyable.

If customers don't shoot their wad while they are being ridden things usually progress to missionary style. The transition typically involves the service provider climbing down, laying on her back and spreading her legs wide and invitingly.

The service providers are usually quite good at holding their customers back with their legs and arms in what feels like an embrace. In fact this maneuver is really meant to keep the customers from going in them too hard and deep. Considerate and caring guys are most appreciated by service providers since they can control themselves instead of being controlled. At the end of the day sex is a job for the women working these places. They want to avoid undue stress on themselves and their private parts.

Customers will usually only be given doggy style access if they directly request it during sex. If they do that they still may be denied though they usually are not. Guys who go crazy and start pounding away are by all accounts not warmly received. Many of the service providers who work at massage parlors are rather tight in the vaginal region even though they bang guys on a regular basis. They don't want to ruin the goods that they use to make a living or feel pain. Considerate guys along with any person with a functioning brain can understand this.

After customers shoot their loads the service providers grab their junk by the base and pull it out ensuring that the rubber stays on and no seed is spilled. Then the service providers gently remove the condom and put a wet towel over the still pulsating penis. As the customers kick back and relax the providers leave the room and come back with a warm wet towel to gently clean things up.

Most sessions wind up with some small talk. The service providers usually help their customers get dressed too. Mileage will vary here even with the same girl. Sometimes they want to lie together and cuddle with customers and sometimes they want to get the guy out the door as soon as possible. A customer may be thanked and offered a drink or candy by the mamasan on the way out, or he may not see anything but the door. Generally speaking the nicer customers are more likely to receive better service in the future.

It really is as simple as that. A guy makes an appointment, goes in, has a good time with a hot girl, and then leaves. That's one of the reason these places are so common and popular.

As it stands Korean massage parlors tend to be some of the most reliable adult oriented shops in the country. On top of that they often employ some of the most attractive women of any business of their kind. That doesn't seem set to change anytime soon despite the wishes of some in the anti-sex brigade.

These are general overviews and not iron clad rules. There are always exceptions. On top of the many legitimate massage parlors owned by Koreans or Chinese people where no sexual service are offered, there are also other types of venues around.

For example, in a few locations Korean owned massage parlors may only offer the same kind of hands-on extras most common to Chinese shops, or something more exotic like the soapy body slide. There are also Chinese owned massage parlors where full sex is offered to customers.

Russian massage parlors in the United States aren't nearly as common as their Chinese or Korean counterparts, but where they exist they are pretty straightforward about the services they offer. These shops mainly seem to exist in New York and the Philadelphia area, but I have also seen a few elsewhere.

It's not too tough to figure out whether or not a place is Russian. For one, they usually advertise as such. Even when they don't, it doesn't take a whole lot of brain power to figure out that a place staffed with blond women with names like Svetlana and Olga who speak accented English is probably Russian.

Russian massage parlors may also employ women from the sphere of the former Soviet Union. That means that Belorussian, Kazakh, Ukrainian, and women from a host of other areas may be the ones giving customers their "Russian" rub downs. While the nationalities of the masseuses has little bearing on the services provided it does still seem to be in some way relevant to any report on the subject.

Russian massage parlors in the United States are somewhat rare and little seen. Besides being few and far between, they typically stick to advertising through select avenues and are less likely to appear on review websites.

At the same time, many Russian massage parlors are oriented to sexual services almost completely. Some may even describe them as being closer to brothels than massage shops.

Most Russian massage parlors of an adult nature require customers to make appointments before visiting. There's usually no other option especially for first time customers as the majority of these places do not even advertise their locations publicly.

The rates for sex at Russian massage parlors are usually between 160 and 200 US dollars. Customers looking to pay for such activities normally book a one hour session on their first visit. They then hand over all of the money for the sessions which is normally all that is required by the provider. Some customers do tip on top of the standard fee but the shops themselves don't usually require any additional payment. There are a select few Russian places that ask customers to pay a house fee of something like 50 dollars up front with customers left to negotiate the rest of the payment with the providers in private but even then the total cost usually amounts to about the same 160 to 200 dollars.

Russian massage parlors operate a lot like Korean massage parlors, and also tend to staff attractive women in their early-twenties to mid-thirties. Breast implants are a lot less common at Russian places than Korean places but some providers do sport silicone. At Russian massage parlors showers before and after sessions are sometimes required and sometimes not available at all. Sessions usually start with a very brief, mediocre rubdown and then quickly proceed into sexual activity.

The level of performance at Russian massage parlors

seems to be a bit lower than what customers normally get in Korean massage parlors, but there are big exceptions. Some of the women working in these Russian establishments either get really into it or otherwise deserve Academy Awards for their acting abilities. When no tip is expected these over the top performances can only really be explained by enthusiasm or a wish by providers to satisfy their customers.

Another difference between Korean and Russian massage parlors is the question of oral sex. While the majority of women in Russian massage parlors do perform oral sex on their customers, there are some who do not.

Since oral sex is not something most first time customers or providers can bring up safely it is often not discussed upfront. Because of that customers only find out whether or not oral sex is offered at a particular place or by a specific provider when they go through an actual session. Whether or not oral sex is provided the majority of sessions end up the same way, with condom covered full service.

It should be noted that some of the Russian operations, especially when set up hastily, are basically rip off joints. While there are some no-happy-endings-allowed Chinese massage parlors that try to attract horned up men by running ads containing pictures of sexy Asian models in media outlets where erotic services usually appear, this sort of bait and switch does seem to be more common with Russian places.

Russian massage parlors with no reviews appearing anywhere online would be most likely to do the bait and switch. Guys looking for sexual services in these places may keep upping their tips in the vein hopes of getting something but end up with little more than an expensive back rub. It is not necessarily common, but it's not unheard of either.

American massage parlors are probably the most common massage shops after Chinese massage parlors in the United States.

They tend to be independent massage parlors with names like "Hollywood Massage" and staffs that range from cosmopolitan mixes to those more uniformly white than North Dakota in January.

In some cases these massage parlors are little more than knocking shops in disguise. In other cases they may be upstanding shops with pristine walls decorated with licenses and training certificates in the front and a row of tanning beds set up somewhere in the back. Most fall somewhere in between.

There really is no standard when it comes to these kinds of massage parlors. They may offer hands on happy endings, full service, or nothing extra whatsoever. Services may even differ between individual masseuses in a particular shop. An official prohibition against extra sexual services from the management doesn't stop a lot of women from offering them in private as a way to make extra money.

In some American massage shops happy endings simply don't happen, but aroused guys are invited to finish themselves off. They may even be offered this fantastic "bonus" if, and only if, they promise to tip generously. Some customers enjoy this or are at least able to settle for such limited services. Others look to other venues for more with the idea that they can masturbate themselves at home without spending a dime.

Because of the wide variation that exists between shops and even individual providers I can't give any real average price points for these kinds of American massage parlors. I can say that they tend to ask for higher rates than the women who work in Asian and Russian massage parlors and offer comparable services. Why is that? Perhaps the native-born women who work American massage parlors feel more entitled. Perhaps they are conditioned to expect more by growing up in the richest country in the world. Maybe it's a combination of the two, or not related to either. Who knows?

Some happy ending massage aficionados in the United

States swear by American massage parlors that offer extras. Others avoid them all at all costs sticking to places like Korean and Chinese massage parlors instead.

Most of the customers for these American massage places are probably irregular visitors who either wander in or hear or read something that intrigues them.

After the Chinese, Korean, American and Russian massage parlors, the next most prominent has to be the Thai massage parlor. These places seem to be a lot more common on the West Coast, though they do exist elsewhere. I'm not talking about the American massage shops that may list "Thai massage" as one of their service specialties. I'm speaking of the Thai massage parlors that are owned and operated by Thai people.

Actual Thai massage is a form of reflexology that developed in the country it is named after many years ago. While in Thailand the women working in many massage parlors offer at least some form of happy ending if requested, in the United States the Thai massage parlors seem to tend more toward the "legitimate" side of things. There are no hard and firm rules when it comes to Thai massage parlors. Prices and services vary a lot from one shop to another. For that reason the guys who seek out happy ending massage in these sorts of places usually rely heavily on user reviews they find online or even word of mouth.

In some ways the typical Thai massage parlor in the US will operate like the Chinese massage parlors described earlier. The main difference is that customers will often be asked to put on a sort of silky pajama set before their massage. Another difference is that happy endings are a lot more rare in Thai massage parlors, with few notable exceptions.

Beyond the Thai massage parlors there are a few other ethnically based places around, usually focused around the neighborhoods where people of those ethnicities live.

Greek, Turkish and Russian spas are normally not places

where any kind of happy ending service is served up. In some cases male customers go to these places to get intense therapeutic massages from other men. Other times they are places where guys search out other men to have anonymous sex with. Happy endings from women aren't offered.

Beyond the realm of massage, there are also a number of specialized shops around that cater to specific ethnic enclaves in the United States. These range from Vietnamese cafes in California where scantly clad and sexy women in their twenties with big breasts dance around topless and occasionally even give big tippers a few strokes under a table to Japanese piano bars and private Korean hostess clubs where the servers are rumored to provide customers with blow jobs along with their orders of beer and fresh fruit.

While I do know something about these sorts of places I will not go into too much detail about them here. Those not recognized as members of the ethnic groups these businesses cater to are very unlikely to be accepted as customers. Conversely, those who belong to the groups in question are unlikely to read this book. Suffice it to say that these kinds of places exist.

Tantric massage practitioners offer the surest bet willing customers to get a happy ending massage, though they often have to put up with a healthy does of new age mumbo-jumbo. The ideas behind tantric massage are a mix of various forms of traditional and modern spirituality that are well beyond the scope and subject of this book. In essence, guys who go in for a tantric massage normally receive a very effective and relaxing massage that will often involve at least one orgasm, though sometimes they are restricted to the so-called "dry orgasm" which is sort of ruined orgasm that stops short of ejaculation.

Originating in India quite some time ago, Tantric massage emerged in North America in the 1960's and 70's with the counterculture. Today, it is usually on offer in the biggest cities where it is most often practiced by independent individuals or groups of two in small spaces and private homes. Some tantric masseuses will also travel to the homes or hotels of their customers. Tantric practitioners advertise in all sorts of places, often right alongside more mainstream masseuses who may or may not scorn the idea of tantra all together.

Tantric practitioners often utilize their own detailed websites to find new customers too. A quick Google search can bring up countless tantric masseuses.

Tantric massage often involves things like music and candles, and a little bit of back and forth. The service provider, who may refer to herself by some Tantra jargon like "Dakini" rather than "masseuse," will normally try to tailor each session to the perceived needs of the client.

Customers of tantric masseuses can expect things like breathing instruction and the like alongside the rubdown. Wraps and body scrubs may also be on the menu. Long, extended periods of erotic enjoyment will typically be included in the session even when it is billed as a sort of spiritual or even medical healing. The goal for tantric providers seems to be to prolong things. Depending on the customers, the session booked and the service provider, those undergoing a tantric massage might be brought to climax one or several times, or alternatively not at all.

Tantric massage practitioners take their craft and the philosophy behind it very seriously. Customers who visit tantric practitioners either have to play along with the whole ordeal or lay back in silence while enjoying the finer aspects of the art if they want to complete a session. Guys who show up to a tantric session talking about happy endings and blowing loads, or anything similar, are much more likely to be shown the door than a good time.

Tantric massage typically costs much more than any of the other happy ending massage options in the US. There is no set rate that applies across the board, but sessions often cost between 375 to 500 dollars an hour. Longer sessions are available, and recommended by practitioners, though the price continues to go up in correlation with the extension of time. The biggest advocates of tantric massage are known to suggest sessions of three hours or more though such appointments can cost one upwards of a thousand bucks.

Unlike massage parlors where customers can book as little as an hour before a session or even just walk in, those who want a tantric massage typically need to make reservations much further in advance. Some tantric service providers even want to talk a bit or meet potential customers for an "introduction session" before agreeing to any booking. As might be expected, those who are more laid back and easy going are more likely to get the kinds of services they seek.

Couples and women looking for massage with release find that nearly every tantric masseuse will gladly take them on as customers and provide the services they are looking for. The service is sometimes given a different name like "yoni massage" but the end result is the same.

There are also a few masseuses in the United States that operate under titles like "sexologist" or "sexual health instructor." They do things much in the same way as their self-proclaimed tantric counterparts except that may they work from a basis of education rather than spirituality. Still, rates and services can be very similar.

Masseuses who use terms like "sensual instructor" usually fall somewhere between the two.

For whatever reason, those who provide tantric massage, sensual instruction and like usually operate much more in the open than some of the other masseuses who provide extra services. My only guess is that since they base their practice on ideas of spirituality and education, they feel they are immune from laws designed to curb the sale sexual services.

Tantric massage may be more tolerated than other forms

of sensual or sexual massage in the US because it couches itself in spiritual or holistic terms. This can be viewed as being something like head shops in the US that sell water pipes and the like. Customers who enter those places talking about marijuana are often refused service even though everyone more or less knows that no one smokes tobacco through a bong.

In any event the billing of tantra as a holistic practice seems to work. As far as I can tell, few are ever prosecuted for offering tantric massage or hands-on sexual instruction in the United States. The same can not be said for other erotic massage providers.

I should also mention traveling or "outcall" masseuses in the United states. They may operate under any number of titles, and as independent individuals or as staff members of larger organized operations. They tend to advertise in the same kinds of places as escorts, and there's a very good reason for that.

Most of the women advertising offers of outcall, erotic or sensual massage are simply selling full service sex. This may or may not be proceeded by an actual massage, but even when it is, the massage rendered isn't typically of the type that would offer much in the form of pain relief.

Some of these traveling ladies do not offer full service, or at least do not offer it in all situations. These masseuses are more likely to show up with folding massage tables and oils and consider their work to be more on the therapeutic than sexual side of things.

Guys who call traveling masseuses they find in ads and ask about things like extra sexual services or happy endings are usually not given the time of day. In what is a largely hostile world these traveling ladies put in a lot of effort to protect themselves.

Those men who actually expect to meet the women in question are usually much more demure and simply go with the flow of things rather than engaging in any explicit conversation.

Traveling masseuses who advertise alongside escorts and visit customers in their private residences or hotel rooms at all hours of the day and night often do offer sensual services.

Those who charge rates of 200 dollars or more per hour and more likely to offer full service than just happy endings by hand.

Masseuses who do outcall to customer's rooms and show up at one o'clock in the morning wearing revealing mini skirts with no massage supplies are probably most likely to be escorts who offer little or no massage at all.

I chose my words carefully when I say "most likely." You'll notice that I do not say anything about sureties or guarantees. If as they say there are no guarantees in life, there certainly aren't any when it comes to erotic massage.

Obviously, and to repeat what was written earlier in this book, these are generalities. There are absolutely mainstream masseuses who visit clients in their homes, charge high rates, and do not offer sensual or sexual services of any kind.

Sexual services are not only sold in strip clubs, massage parlors, and on the streets of the United States. There are other sex shops around too, even if most people remain blissfully unaware of their presence.

In some areas, Latin ballerina bars are common. While many may not be aware of these places they do exist in some numbers. Good examples of this type of place can be found around Queens Boulevard and Roosevelt Avenue in the New York borough of Queens.

To the untrained eye these places probably look like regular bars that just happen to be popular with Latinos. The only features that might set them apart would be things like frosted windows, security guards posted outside, or signs hanging in front that say things like "dancers wanted" in Spanish.

Ballerina bars in the United States operate somewhat like the aforementioned hostess bars in Asia. Most customers are immigrants from Central America who work long hours far from home visit these bars to dance with the Latina women on staff.

Ladies who work in these bars range in looks and age. In a single bar there may be immigrants from Central and South America along with women born to Dominican parents in the United States. Some ladies are twenty years old with near perfect bodies while others are older with short stocky frames.

Drinks are sold to customers as they are in any other bar. Customers can also buy lady drinks for the staff if they so desire. These drinks are sold at double or triple the normal price, with the extra profits being split between the bar and the worker.

When customers want to dance with one of the women working in the bar they simply ask. They are normally accepted with the expectation that tips will be given.

Depending on the bar, customers can give the ladies as little as $1 per song to dance with them. In other cases, such as when the women furious grind their backsides on the groins of excited customers while upbeat reggaeton music plays, tips may be as much as ten dollars per song.

The ballerina bars are not purely dens of prostitution but customers have been known to negotiate discreetly with individual women with some frequency and success. Repeat customers familiar to the women in the bars seem to be more successful at negotiating for extra activities than others.

Last but certainly not least, I must mention the underground brothels that exist all over the United States. There's not much to detail about these places, but they deserve to be covered in the interests of accuracy.

American brothels are places where customers have sex with women for a set amount of money. That's basically all there is to it.

Customers find these places through word of mouth or internet reviews. The days when they were found through newspaper ads have mostly ended except in the cases of foreign language papers published in languages like Spanish and Chinese where discrete advertisements are still published with some regularity.

Customers either call these places for an appointment or simply rock up to the door. They often operate out of private apartments or houses and they don't tend to stay in any one location for long. Raids and closures are common.

The prices at these kinds of places are usually among the lowest of any organized sex shop in the US. The services and surroundings typically reflect the lower rates with worn out rooms and disinterested service providers being the norm.

Some regular participants in the sex industry describe these sorts of places as "blow and go" or "pump and dump" venues which despite the crudity paints a pretty accurate picture.

The United States is one of the largest, most populous, and most prosperous countries in the world. A somewhat large commercial sex industry exists in the country but most of it is officially outlawed and thus underground at least to some degree. The small regulated legal prostitution market that exists doesn't seem to have put a dent into the pockets of unofficial sex workers even when they operate in the same areas.

Many men continue to pay for sex in the United States. Others pay for sex when they travel abroad to places where such services are more readily available. Still more avoid the commercial sex industry entirely or limit themselves to the more socially acceptable realms of strip clubs and porn.

2. Japan

Japan may very well have the largest commercial sex industry in the world. This *fuzoku* exists all over the country, and in many cases is totally legal.

The sale of vaginal intercourse is specifically outlawed in Japan, but nothing is said about other sex acts in the law. So totally legal sex shops and providers offer services like hand jobs, blow jobs and even anal sex openly and routines. There are also others who offer full vaginal sex through legal loopholes or by skirting the law.

The Japanese equivalent of the escort comes in the form of "health" outfits. Delivery health shops send women out to meet customers. They're basically escort agencies offering outcall. Fashion health shops run a similar way but either have rooms on site for customers to use or they utilize rooms in nearby love hotels which can be hired out by the hour. Prices can range from 10,000 to 80,000 Yen ($90-720 USD).

A handful of out and out escort agencies due exist, but they aren't nearly as common as the aforementioned deli helu businesses. The escort agencies that do exist usually aim for foreign customers and charge premium prices.

Image clubs are a little rarer. They operate like health shops except that they offer all kinds of fetish services ranging from costume and bondage play to erotic adult breast feeding. There are also many similar shops around such as maid cafes and girls bars, which do not provide actual sexual services.

Illegal Korean delivery health and *estute* shops can be found all over Japan. They might publicly advertise massage only but in fact they are known for offering sex. As the name would indicate these shops are often staffed by Korean or

Chinese women. As you might expect, they are also shut down with regularity. Fees are usually around 12,000 Yen ($108 USD).

Some Thai and Chinese massage parlors are known mainly for offering hand jobs, though they are given along with massage and table showers. These places may be technically illegal but they are not shut down very often. Prices are usually around 10,000 Yen.

Another type of massage parlor more or less specializes in happy endings. Staffed by women from places like Thailand, these shops offer a mid-range body massage that finishes with a hand job from a fully clothed provider. Asia Relax in Kabukicho is maybe the most famous shop of this kind. It charges 9,000 Yen for an oil massage and hand job.

Strip clubs are somewhat common in Japan. The Japanese "strip theater" model is different than what is found in other countries. Customers pay an entrance fee then sit around a stage where dancers do elaborate performances that end with them spreading their legs fully nude. The people in the audience clap but aren't expected to tip. Customers can usually pay money after a performance to take a picture with the nude dancers. Some of these strip clubs used to sell services like blow jobs from the dancers too, but those days seem to be over. A handful of western style strip clubs exist too. They are comparatively expensive and do not offer sexual services.

The sort of peep shows described earlier in this book exist but are not very common. Customers watch women dance nude from private booths and have the option to pay extra for hand jobs or blow jobs after the performances. New Hot Point in the Shinjuku section of Tokyo is one of the better-known facilities of this type. Admission and a hand job usually costs around 4,200 Yen ($38 USD).

Compensated dating abounds in Japan. Some credit Japan as creating the entire concept, though in reality the practice existed throughout history in different forms.

Nowadays websites are probably the most common places for people to arrange compensated dating, but brick and mortar shops also exist. There are many dating cafes around the country where women go to meet guys who then offer them money to spend time together or have sex in a nearby love hotel. Kirari Community Cafes are maybe the best known businesses of this type. There are also clubs set up for compensated dating with huge databases of women for men to comb through. Universe Club is one of the largest clubs of this type in Japan, and it even has an English section to deal with foreign customers. The money spent varies quite a bit from one person to the next.

Oppai pubs are places where guys pay to play with tits. *Oppai* is the Japanese word for breasts, and pub means more or less the same thing in Japan as it does everywhere else.

Customers pay a set fee to enter an oppai pub then either sit or lay next to a series of women over a certain period of time. Kissing and touching above the waste is usually permitted while any touching below the belt is forbidden. Oppai pubs are quite common especially in Tokyo. A normal entrance fee for 40 minutes is 5000 Yen ($45 USD).

Red light districts aren't as common as they used to be in Japan, but still exist. Matsushima Shinchi and Tobita Shinchi in Osaka are two of the most well known. The women in these districts kneel on pillows in open shop houses waiting for customers. Oral and full sex is offered in small rooms on premises for 11,000 Yen.

Supposedly these red light districts are older than laws against prostitution so they are not bothered by law enforcement. I don't know whether or not that is actually the case, but in any event these places are well known and open to the public and they rarely seem to face any problems from the law.

Soaplands are probably the most well known of all the sex shops in Japan. It is thought that the soapy massage parlors in Thailand and some of the Chinese sex saunas base themselves on soaplands.

Soaplands are basically bath houses for men where sexually services are offered. They have a long history in Japan. The ancient Yoshiwara district of Tokyo was filled with prostitution as early as 1617. Today it is lined with many soaplands.

The theory is that guys go to soaplands to be washed by women (soaplands were originally called *toruko buro* in Japan, in reference to Turkish baths). The reality is that customers are usually bathed and given sex for a set fee.

Depending on the amount of time customers book they can also receive a soapy body to body slide on an inflatable mat when visit a soapland. This *nuru nuru* (slippery) massage has become popular around the world now, probably thanks to Japanese porn and the internet.

Soaplands range from the low rent places staffed by middle aged moms to the high end places staffed by famous porn stars that give customers free rides in luxury cars. Some places are even known for offering unprotected sex as a normal part of service. Prices at soaplands can be anywhere from 20,000 to 110,000 Yen ($180- 000 USD).

Japan's blow job bar scene is perhaps the most notorious. At the very least, it's the most widespread. In parts of the Tokyo megalopolis, and a number of other areas around the country, these "pink salons" (or pinsaros) are ubiquitous.

Officially licensed as restaurants, these shops offer oral sex to customers for relatively low rates. Customers pay 2000 Yen ($18 USD) or more when they enter. Then they're led to one of many semi-private booths in a more or less open room. They are services in those booths in site of everyone by women who can range from full nude twenty year old gals to elderly women in house frocks.

These shops are known as being on the low end of the sex industry. Sometimes they offer "two-for-one" specials or even membership reward cards to get customers. It's not uncommon for a pink salon regular to have a card in his wallet that allows him one free blow job for every ten he purchases at his favorite suck shop.

Once in a while a cut-rate pink salon will run a sale so enticing that men will literally line up in the street waiting for their shot with the blow job providers inside.

There are many blow job bars in Tokyo. Only a handful of them are known to accept foreigners, and those have some of the worst reputations among Japanese men who frequent pink salons. Jan Jan in the Sugamo area and Hanamaru in Kabukicho are probably the best examples.

In fact most sex shops and providers in Japan do not accept foreigners, especially foreigners who don't speak Japanese. Various reasons are given for this. One is that foreigners can't understand the sometimes complicated rules in sex shops. Another is plain old xenophobia which can run rife in the land of the rising sun.

Nowadays there are some commercial sex providers who will accept foreigners on an individual basis. Recently some shops have eve opened that actually orient themselves to foreigners entirely.

3. South Korea

Korea has a history of sexual service providers going back to days before the founding of the USA was even a dream in anyone's head. Since the Second World War the industry has been further shaped and influenced by the changes that have taken place, but it has never come close to being eliminated.

There is not a city or town in South Korea that doesn't contain some sort of prostitution or sex shop. The variety is vast. There are coffee delivery shops that send women to customer's homes for sex and coffee shops where sex is offered right inside. There are many red light districts and brothels. There are Karaoke parlors where female attendants get nude and offer blow jobs and even full sex to all the male customers in attendance. There are *aparta-hotel* and room salon incall sex shops and fetish clubs. There are kiss bangs and lip cafes where customers pay to kiss women and get blow jobs. There are large sex saunas called *anma* and countless double pole barbershops where men can purchase oral or vaginal sex. There are also all the other kinds of things you might expect including escorts and happy ending massage parlors.

In fact, you can hardly walk down a street in South Korea without passing by one variety or another of commercial sex shop, although you probably won't realize it if you don't speak Korean and aren't familiar with the culture.

The coffee based shops are mostly limited to older men nowadays. In that they resemble the tea rooms in Taiwan locally referred to as "grandpa shops" where older men go to meet working women.

Karaoke parlors visited by Korean men are formally open to the public though semi-secret activity is common inside. Guys often visit in groups and are accompanied by women on staff. Once drinks are passed around things often get sexual and in some places it is even a matter of course that everyone will receive oral sex before the night is through. Guys often pay quite a lot of money when they visit these venues but in many cases it is covered by corporate accounts.

Red light districts can be found in large and small cities. Most of them look like the famous De Wallen red light district in Amsterdam where women stand in red lit windows looking for customers, but a few have older mangers who invite passersby into private rooms to select from available sex providers. Famous red light districts include Cheongnyangni 588, Cheonho and Miari Texas in Seoul as well as Green Street in Busan.

Many red light workers in South Korea will not accept foreign customers. Some say they fear diseases or large penises. Others say Korean guys don't want to follow foreigners and won't visit with a prostitute known for servicing foreigners. Still others say Koreans are just xenophobic and racist.

Perhaps as a result of the common rejection of foreigners in red light districts a place now known as Hooker Hill in the Itaewon section of Seoul sprung up several years ago. There women sit in small bars waiting for foreign guys to walk by. When they see a foreign guy they come out into the street and try their best to tempt him. If a guy enters the doors are locked and he is offered oral and vaginal sex for prices that start at around 70,000 Won ($60 USD).

Anma are the soaplands of South Korea. They are large massage parlors where men pay 280,000 Won ($250 USD) for a table shower, massage, blow job and full sex. They operate a lot like Korean massage parlors in the United States. A major difference is that most of them do not accept customers who are not Korean.

More expensive setups in hotels and apartments are even

less likely to accept foreigners. Some don't even advertise. They operate in the underground and are usually visited by Korean men with money. Some staff women as attractive as K-Pop Idols, at times because the women are actually such stars trying to make extra money on the side.

Many other sex massage parlors that bill themselves as sports massage or simply *massaji* operate like Korean massage parlors too, complete with table showers and sex. They use smaller and less luxurious buildings and charge 180,000 Won ($160 USD) on average. These shops tend to staff middle aged women who are very hardened and mechanical but for whatever reason they are more likely to accept foreign clients. Several places of this kind are located on the small island of Unseo near the Incheon International Airport.

Thai massage parlors are common in South Korea but unlike their counterparts in other parts of the world they almost never seem to offer any sexual services.

Slightly less common are the happy ending massage parlors a large number of which are located in the Gangam section of Seoul. Now widely known because of that annoying pop-dance, Gangnam is an upscale area of the South Korean capital that is home to a number of golf accessory shops, cafes and sex shops.

Happy ending massage parlors charge between 70,000 and 120,000 Won ($60-110 USD). After showering, customers at these parlors are treated to a rotation of regular therapeutic massages from women in their thirties and forties and happy ending massages that conclude with hand jobs or oral sex delivered by attractive women in their twenties. In some places the twenty year old even get topless.

Kiss rooms and lip cafes are somewhat underground. Most are located behind locked doors and on the upper floors of buildings. They advertise online and through word of mouth and in some cases require customers to call over the phone for access. Prices are typically around 50,000 Won ($45 USD).

There are also plenty of independent escorts and escort agencies in South Korea. Their prices can vary greatly. The internet is their main avenue for advertisement but some post up ads on the street and in hotels too.

4. China

China is one the largest countries in the world. It has some of the harshest laws on the books against prostitution but in practice it is fairly widespread.

Chinese sex saunas probably originated in the country, but today they are not as common as they were just a few years ago. The massive concentration of these saunas in Dongguan fell apart in 2014 after local tycoon Liang Yaohui and 1,000 others were arrested. Yaohui was subsequently sentenced to life in prison.

Today sex saunas are spread out and underground. They still need to find customers though, so they usually advertise in some way or another. It's typical for a sauna located in the basement of a skyscraper or hotel to have male staff wandering around the lobby asking guys if they're looking for massage.

Chinese sex saunas operate like any others. In mainland China rates at these saunas start at 750 Yuan ($110 USD) and go up from there.

Independents and escort agencies abound in China. Sometimes they are arrested. Other times they are left alone for extended periods of time. Prices greatly range from one person to the next.

More common are happy ending massage parlors which come in various forms. Some look like massage parlors while others are set up like barbershops. The women inside are usually of average looks. They tend to offer things like blow job for around 300 Yuan ($45 USD).

In some parts of the country there are Chinese prostitutes who work well known streets and other public areas.

They serve customers for little money, usually in dirty rooms or even outside. They are the local equivalent of the streetwalker, and they can be quite popular.

There are also some well known bars where freelancers go to find customers. Women from countries like Vietnam are actually more common in these places than Chinese women. Customers come from China and all over the world. Most women selling sex at Manhattan want 1000 Yuan ($145 USD). Manhattan in Shanghai was one of the most well known bars of this kind until it shut down in 2017. The similar Judy's in the same city is still in business.

Prostitution in China is widespread but it is not in your face. Things are a lot different in the Special Administrative Regions where the sale of sex is still permitted.

5. Hong Kong

While plenty of guys in Hong Kong score sex for free on a regular basis, many also pay for their pleasure. With such an abundance of sex providers around it is not to difficult to understand them.

Although Hong Kong is now officially a part of China, sex work remains legal in the Special Administrative Region under the "one country, two system" principle.

Perhaps most accessible of all sex providers are the countless women who sell sex out of "walk ups" or "one woman brothels." These are more or less what they sound like. Women set up shop in small apartments and sell sex to guys who come.

There is only one woman in each room. This is due to a law that allows the sale of sex but bans pimping. Similar laws exist elsewhere. Women don't team up when these laws exist because they don't want to be accused of pimping or anything similar.

Many of the gals who who work one woman brothels advertise themselves on websites like the well known Sex141. Other sites like Miss148 and 161sex are also commonly used. For whatever reason Chinese women usually use real pictures while Thai women who work the apartment brothels often do not.

Still other women don't advertise at all. Instead they just wait for guys to come knock on their doors. They mostly operate out of places like the infamous Fuji Building on Lockhart Road. Since customers come through all day knocking on doors to see who is available, they don't feel the need to post advertisements online.

Chinese women are most common in the walk up brothels but Thais and even the occasional Russian can also be found. Typical prices at one woman brothels in Hong Kong are 300-500 Hong Kong Dollars ($40-65 USD) for a quick session that includes uncovered oral followed by condom covered intercourse.

These walk ups are commonly but they are hardly the be all and end all of prostitution in Hong Kong. There are also plenty of independents and escort agencies along with a fair number of streetwalkers who are commonly found in areas like Wan Chai and Yau Ma Tei's Temple Street.

Somewhere between the dating circuit and the straight forward sex industry are the freelancers of the Wan Chai bar scene. On certain nights a concentration of bars in this part of the city is filled with overworked domestic helpers usually from the Philippines and Indonesia looking for some fun and some extra money to go with it. They are accompanied by the girls sell sex exclusively, even though those full-timers often claim to be domestic helpers too.

With names like Neptunes and New Makati, the places in Wan Chai are basically regular bars where sex workers ply their trade. They meet with guys who come to bars to find sex usually expecting to use Hong Kong Dollars as a sort of social lubricant.

The going rate in this area is 500-1000 HKD ($65-130 US dollars), usually given by the men the morning after the sex and sleeping with little to no discussion. Only the most hardened pros typically negotiate exact prices upfront and in advance of any sex.

There are also some bars in Wan Chai that follow a go go bar model. They aren't as common but there are plenty around. The Filipina and Thai women who work the bars wear bikinis and have sex with customers outside for a set amount of money. Prices are negotiable but most customers and dancers seem to settle on a number somewhere around 1500 HKD ($191 USD).

As you might expect, Hong Kong is also home to a number of Chinese massage parlors. I've written about Chinese massage parlors in the United States earlier. The Hong Kong version isn't much different.

Some of these parlors are small and dingy. Others are nicer and often located inside of hotels. Some are even high class spas.

There are no Chinese sex saunas with line ups of women offering full service, but some of the spas are large and well appointed.

Typical services offered in these places are hand jobs and oral sex. Some places do offer full service, but that's usually done discreetly. In the regular massage parlors hand jobs can be tacked on at the end as an extra or promoted right up front as "lingam massage" and listed on a menu. Prices range depending on the place but can be anywhere from 250 HKD ($32 USD) on up.

One of the most well known and longest running spas for men in Hong Kong is K-Pressure on Woosung Street. Hand job massages have been provided by the many pretty women on staff there for years at a rate of around 500 HKD.

6. Macau

The sale of sexual services in legal in Macau, which is probably one of the reasons why there are so many well-organized and sanitary commercial sex venues in the small island city.

Sex workers in Macau have access to free health services which includes testing for sexually transmitted disease. In 2012 Vicky Lei Wai Kei from the Health Bureau of Macau publicly stated that "no HIV positive case was found among the women" she had access to, even though those women tended to come from the less organized and more inexpensive side of the local sex industry.

Although the Macau SAR is quite small and compact it contains numerous people and places offering sexual services. Unlike Japan and South Korea, the scene in Macau is totally open to foreign visitors and there's no real barrier for those who don't speak the local language since multilingual people from all over the world are commonly on staff. There does seem to be prejudice against certain skin colors and national origins in some places though it doesn't exist everywhere.

Chinese sex saunas are the most well known and prominent venues in Macau. There are dozens around including well known places like Rio and Emperor.

As previously described these saunas offer everything from bathing and blow jobs from twenty year old shower attendants to ear cleanings, dick and ball massages, and of course full service sex.

Customers spend as much time as they'd like in the saunas. It's not out of the norm for customers to sleep in the large lounge chairs or over in special sleeping areas that come complete with beds. Unlimited food and drink is on offer too, usually for free.

Rates vary depending on the place, the services and the level and origin of the girls a customer chooses to spend time with, but on average customers probably spend the equivalent of between 250 and 500 US dollars for several hours inside a sauna with one or two orgasms.

Karaoke parlors or KTVs cater exclusively to Chinese and Asian men who are used to the model. It's the same as anywhere else in Asia. Guys spend a lot of money to book a room that comes complete with female attendants. At some point they can try to negotiate payment for sex. The women are free to reject their proposals but the reality is that a lot of paid sex arrangements come out of these places in Macau every day.

Fishbowl massage parlors aren't as common in Macau as saunas but there are a few around. These fishbowls operate like the fishbowl massage and soapy massage parlors in Thailand and Cambodia.

Customers walk in, chose one or more of the seated ladies, and then head to a private room where they get bath play followed by full service sex. The price for a standard session is usually 1749 Patacas ($215 USD).

There are a few brothels in Macau. They operate like most other brothels around the world. They are straight forward "point and poke" places. Customers walk in, select a woman or take whoever is next in line, head to a private room, take a shower then receive a blow job and protected sex. The women who work the brothels are usually Vietnamese or Chinese ladies in their twenties and thirties. Prices average around 888 Patacas ($110 USD).

Casino gals are more common than brothels to be sure. These are basically freelancers who prowl the many casinos in Macau looking for customers. They work in hotel rooms and charge a thousand Patacas or more. Most of them only speak

Cantonese or Mandarin as they tend to hail from mainland China and mostly work with Chinese customers.

For years there was a constant rotation of Chinese sex workers in the basement of the Lisboa Hotel. They always moved around to avoid the security guards. They moved so fast in fact that the place came to be referred to as the "Lisboa Racetrack." Eventually it came to an end in 2015 when a major hotel boss and a hundred suspected prostitutes were rounded up in a raid.

Of course that raid didn't eliminate prostitutes. Most of them now just set up in hotel rooms or apartments and use things like the "find people around me" feature on the Whatsapp smart-phone application to find customers.

These women can overlap with the limited local population of escorts. Both use the same avenues to find customers. Websites carry some listings but activity is moving more towards phone apps now.

Some of the women who work at jobs like locker attendant and waitress in the sex saunas even supplement their incomes by meeting customers after work. This isn't allowed officially so they have to be discreet about passing on their contact information.

Other women go to local nightclubs for fun and consider any extra arrangements to be paid for sex just a bonus. The amounts of money paid for these activities have too great a range to be nailed down.

Walk up brothels are pretty rare in Macau. Where they exist they operate in the same way as the previously described one woman brothels across the water in Hong Kong. Rates are similar too.

7. Taiwan

Depending on who you ask, Taiwan is either its own country, the "real China," or an independent island country. In practice it functions as most other countries complete with laws against prostitution. In practice those laws are routinely broken and ignored.

Sex is sold all over Taiwan. Taipei gives the best examples. As the capital of Taiwan you might expect that.

There is a large local sex industry in Taipei but it is not necessarily visible to the untrained eye. There are no go go bar complexes with half naked women calling in customers but the city is home to a lot of places offering sexual services.

Escorts are very popular for locals and visitors alike. There are many local escorts in Taipei. They mainly find their clients through online advertisements posted on websites. The same goes for foreign escorts who sometimes stop by Taipei to ply their trade while traveling through the region.

Taiwan doesn't have nearly as many massage parlors as nearby places like Bangkok or Ho Chi Minh City, but it does contain a lot of shops offering body rubs. Many also offer more to male clients.

Unlike Singapore where "health centers" often offer sexual services, places that call themselves health centers in Taipei are usually completely mainstream shops that don't have anything to do with sex. Places offering full sexual services in Taipei often have "spa" or "sauna" in their names but there are also mainstream spas and saunas.

Caeserworld Sauna is a large and somewhat well known sauna complex for men that has a hidden passage leading to rooms where massage and full service is offered for 4200 Taiwan Dollars ($137 USD). A few other saunas follow a similar model.

Taizhilian Spa is a smaller but just as well known spa-style massage parlor popular with foreigners where a mostly Vietnamese staff offers everything from hand jobs to full service. Prices range from 2000 to 5000 NTD ($65-164 USD).

Many small massage parlors in Taipei have "Thai" in their name but unlike Thai massage parlors in other countries these places do not staff any actual Thai women or even offer Thai massage. A few places with Thai in the name like Thai Happiness and Thai Leisurely Life usually offer hand jobs to customers at the end of oil massage sessions. The expected tip is 1000 NTD ($36 USD).

Some underground blow job bars are reported to exist but if so they are very under the radar. Fluency in the local language may be required to find such establishments, assuming they are still around.

Hostess clubs on the other hand are fairly common. People who do not speak Mandarin might would probably hard time visiting them but they are popular with locals and even travelers and expats from other parts of Asia like Japan with a grasp of the language. These hostess bars are a lot like hostess clubs in Japan. This means they are mainly places for guys to unwind with attractive women. Actual sex is usually not available.

There are not a huge number of street walkers in Taipei but some ladies do stand around looking for customers. Lin Shan North Road is one of the most common places for street walkers to stroll. The area is also home to a number of other adult related businesses.

There are also many KTV or karaoke centers in Taipei. They operate as KTVs all over Asia do. A staff of women provides entertainment to customers who pay for use of the rooms as well as any drinks or food they purchase. Customers are expected to tip the women for their services. Some of the women will leave the KTVs with customers to have sex with cash but others will not.

Many of the biggest and most popular KTVs in Taipei are located around Linsen North Road. This is also a popular area for touts to seek out customers for their shops. Women sometimes work this area for customers too.

In both Linsen and the old Monga red light district in Wanhua, some of these women try to pull customers into their lounges and tea houses. The main customer base is made up of immigrant workers and older locals which is why these places are often referred to by locals as a gong diam or "grandfather shops."

Monga was a large and open red light district until laws passed in the early 1990's banned the sale of sexual services in Taiwan. Recently however there has been talk of establishing a legal zone for prostitution in Monga, probably in response to the fact that prostitution continues in the area on an underground basis even though it is officially outlawed.

The most notable adult businesses in Taiwan usually don't offer sex at all. I'm talking about the famed betel nut beauties.

Clad in revealing lingerie and bikinis, these women work small stands in the street. They sell betel nut (*areca catechu*) chew to male customers who are mainly truck drivers. Rumors that they do more seem to be mostly untrue.

8. Malaysia

Malaysia has one of the largest Muslim populations in the world. It's also home to a fairly large commercial sex industry that is spread between the major cities and smaller towns in more rural areas.

Brothels are probably the most common type of sex venue in Malaysia outside of the cities. When it comes to urban areas there is more variety. The capital city of Kuala Lumpur with its large Chinese population has the largest local commercial sex scene in the country.

The city is littered with run of the mill massage parlors though the numbers don't approach those of cities like Bangkok and Pattaya where every street seems to have places pushing massage.

Many of the massage parlors in Kuala Lumpur offer hands-on happy endings for tips though there are places that do not. The largest concentration of massage parlors is on Changkat Bukit Bintang. Masseuses from all over Asia stand out in the street there day and night trying to get people into the various massage shops. Anything from a hand job to full service can be offered to customers by these ladies, though obviously not every masseuse makes such services available.

The various men's spas in Kuala Lumpur follow a familiar pattern. Customers enter and are shown a lineup of the available service providers who tend to be attractive. The ladies are variously Chinese, Vietnamese, Thai, Uzbek, Indonesian or even Malay.

Sessions in these spas typically involve little to no actual massage. Instead customers are showered then given a blow job followed by full service sex. Prices for standard services range between 230 and 300 Ringgit ($56-74 USD).

On top of the more sexually oriented spas there are also countless mainstream and Thai massage parlors around. Many of the Thai massage parlors have black tinted glass and lock their doors in between customers. Many of the same places also offer hand jobs for 50 Ringgit ($12 USD) on top of the regular massage price of 60 Ringgit ($15 USD) per hour.

Kuala Lumpur is also home to a number of freelancers who come into the country from places like Vietnam and the Philippines on tourist visas in search of some quick cash. These freelancers can be found all around with a quite a few using dating website and smart-phone applications to meet potential clients during the day, even though they may not be explicit about their search for cash.

At night certain clubs fill up with these ladies who are looking more for money than a good time. The Beach Club and the Thai Club are the two most well known venues in the city where these women gather every night of the week. They usually ask customers for 300 to 600 Ringgit ($73-$146 USD) for sex.

Street walkers from China and other parts of Asia also ply their trade on Jalan Bukit Bintang throughout the day and night. When the sun is up a few dozen women and a lot more ladyboys can usually be found standing in front of the hotels and marts on the north side of the street between Jalan Pudu and Jalan Sultan Ismail. When the sun goes down many more women come out in the same area. These gals stand on the sidewalks and wait for guys to approach them or give them "the look." Few will approach men who walk through at full speed and look uninterested but a handful can be slightly aggressive at times. A short romp in a nearby hotel can go for as little as 50 Ringgit ($12 USD) though most women there ask for more.

There are KTVs in the city. They are mostly frequented by Chinese guys and Asian businessmen. They operate just like karaoke parlors in other countries. Prices are comparatively high.

Last but not least are the low cost brothels. They are oriented towards locals with little cash like laborers and staffed by older Indian and Chinese women. The Indian women tend more to work out of small rooms while the Chinese women more often work food courts in old rundown malls. Prices are low but the surroundings are dismal. More than one commentator has described these places as dangerous.

9. The Philippines

With a long history of colonialism, foreign guys have been paying for sex in the Philippines for many years. They're joined by millions of local guys who also shell money for sexual services at least once in a while.

Angeles City where US military personal were stationed for years became a well known center of the commercial sex industry in the Philippines. Other cities like Cebu and the capital of Manila are home to a lot of sex workers too.

In Angeles City sex is most commonly sold through the many go go bars located along Fields Avenue and Perimeter Road. The bars on Fields Avenue tend to be larger and more expensive. The bars on Perimeter tend to be smaller and less expensive though they have a reputation for hiring older or less attractive women.

Nude dancing used to be common in Angeles City go go bars. Today is more or less nonexistent even if women do flash their goods from behind their bikinis or bras from time to time.

As with any go go bar customers can buy lady drinks for ladies they want to spend time with. These drinks cost about 250 Pesos ($5 USD).

If a guy wants to take a dancer or other staff member out of a bar, he has to pay a bar fine of anywhere between 1800 and 4000 Pesos ($34-75 USD). This bar fine is all inclusive though some customers do tip on top of it.

In the past it was assumed that all dancers would stay overnight with any customers who paid their bar fine. Today women are more likely to leave after a short round of sex. Regulars in Angeles City call this "pulling a runner."

Not every dancer will leave the bar with every guy who asks. Some only leave with certain guys. Some don't leave at all. Ultimately it's up to the dancers themselves though few guys seem unable to find ladies in the city considering how many bars and dancers are there.

In the past the bars on two short roads called Santos and Ramos were known as "blow row." The women in these bars were known to give blow jobs and have sex on premises for as little as 500 Pesos ($10 USD). Things have changed. Nowadays the ladies in the few remaining bars on these roads require customers to pay a 1000 Peso ($18 USD) bar fine and take them to a nearby hotel if they want sex. Blow jobs are still sometimes given in quiet bars but it is no longer a standard service anywhere.

Massage parlors on Fields Avenue close at night and usually don't offer any sexual services. Some out of the way massage parlors and traveling masseuses will do happy endings for 500 Pesos on top of their normal massage fee.

There are a few karaoke parlors in Angeles City. Some are set up in the typical Asian style and cater to Japanese, Chinese and Korean guys. Others are open to everyone. The Asian style places are most likely to staff women.

There are also a few nightclubs in Angeles City. High Society in particular fills up with hundreds of freelance prostitutes every night. These ladies typically ask 1500 Pesos ($25 USD) for sex.

The many ladies and ladyboys who walk the streets at night normally ask for even less money. It's common for guys to take these street walkers home from places like the Fields Avenue gate for as little as 800 Pesos ($15 USD). There are many stories of theft and even legal trouble floating around from guys who have gone this route, but many others say they regularly pick up Angeles City freelancers from the streets without issue.

Manila also has quite a lot of sex shops and providers. As the capital city of the country you would expect as much. Some of the scene is well known while other aspects are more hidden.

The go go bars in Manila are like those in Thailand. Customers pay a bar fine to take a lady out of a bar then pay additional money to the lady herself for her services. There are no all inclusive bar fines in Manila.

Go go bars are limited to three main areas in Manila. There is P Burgos Street, EDSA, and Ermita.

Ermita is a run down area that probably saw its best days years ago. There are still some bars there concentrated on Del Pilar Street but they aren't on anyone's "must see" lists and they no longer employ dancing girls. The biggest draw for foreigners in the area is the famed LA Cafe. That is not a go go bar but rather a freelancer haunt where women ply their trade. Sex is typically sold for 2000 Pesos.

EDSA is a large closed complex filled with seven go go bars. One owner controls the whole place. Guys go through a metal detector staffed by police when they enter. Inside there are several go go bars staffed with women who dance in bikinis. The bar fine in EDSA is between 1500 and 3000 Pesos ($28-56 USD). The women themselves expect an additional payment of 3000 Pesos for a blow job and sex.

P Burgos is a long narrow street in the Makati section of the city. It has several restaurants along with lots of go go bars. The best looking dancers in the city can be found in these bars, but several older and less attractive ladies work these places too. At Bottoms the women dance in thin suspenders that reveal their breasts but otherwise the women are usually dressed in bikinis in most P Burgos bars. In one bar there is a hidden room in the back where customers are given blow jobs for money.

The bar fine on P Burgos ranges from 2,000 to 8,000 Pesos ($37-160 USD). The women expect an additional 3,000 to 5,000 Pesos for sex. They do not usually stay all night with their customers.

P Burgos is also filled with freelancers and ladyboys at night. These ladies and ladyboys usually propose "massage" to guys who walk up and down the street. In private they often offer sex. These freelancers usually ask 500 Pesos for a massage with any tips for sexual services being negotiable.

There are many karaoke parlors in Manila. As usual they cater most to Asian men. The biggest concentration of these KTVs is located in the Malate area.

Fish bowl massage parlors attached to some of the KTVs and clubs are perhaps more popular. They are staffed with women who offer rudimentary massage and full sex in private rooms.

These massage parlors charge 800 to 3000 Pesos for use of a room. The women expect an additional 1000 to 3000 Pesos for their services.

Some brothels also exist. They cater mostly to locals but they seem to accept anyone who shows up. The quarters used are on the low end of things and prices vary.

Cebu has its own group of go go bars around Mango Square. They don't have the best reputation but some people do sing their praises. This may have something to do with the women of Cebu having a reputation for being among the most beautiful in the country. Cebu is also home to the usual freelancers, brothels and street walkers.

Prostitution can also be found throughout other parts of the country, usually in the form of compensated dating or brothels.

10. Thailand

Thailand probably has the most well known commercial sex industry in the world. The Land of Smiles is home to tens of thousands of sex workers who offer sexual services through many different avenues.

The capital city of Bangkok may have the largest number of sex shops and sex workers in the country. There are go go bars, beer bars, soapy massage parlors, oily massage parlors, Thai massage parlors, blow job bars, fetish bars, street walkers, escorts and freelancers.

Go go bars are centered in four main areas. There is Nana Plaza, Soi Cowboy, Patpong, and Suthisan Road.

Suthisan Road is not known by most foreigners, but there are several go go bars there. Most of the customers inside are Thai. The women dance in bikinis and spend time with customers who buy lady drinks for them. The women usually ask 1,500 Baht ($45 USD) for a short session with sex.

Soi Cowboy is a short road in the middle of Bangkok named after a black guy from America who wore cowboy hats. Today it's a neon alley lined with several go go bars. These bars hire dancers and coyote dancers. The dancers usually work the stage in bikinis. They make money from lady drinks and sex. The coyotes wear skin colored stockings and work for agents. They ask more money for lady drinks and sex than the regular dancers. Some of them don't have sex at all.

There are still some topless and nude dancers on Soi Cowboy, but it's getting less common. Suzy Wong's is known for topless dancers. Crazy House around the corner has lots of full nude ladies on stage and seated around it with customers. A few bars even have women who regularly do hand jobs or blow jobs right in front of everyone. There is also a ladyboy bar on Soi Cowboy called Cockatoos.

Bar fines on Soi Cowboy vary from one bar to another on Soi Cowboy but 600 Baht ($18 USD) is about the norm. The women themselves expect 1500 to 3000 Baht ($45-90 USD) for sex.

Nana Entertainment Plaza on Soi 4 is also known as the NEP. It has a single entrance that leads to a multi-level complex filled with go go bars.

Nana has several ladyboy bars. Most of them are easy to spot. There is one bar called Straps that staffs post-op ladyboys who look quite like natural born women.

Several bars in Nana have at least some topless dancers. Some also have nude dancers in bath tubs where they do shower shows. Coyotes are not common in Nana.

The bar fines in Nana range from 600 to 1000 Baht. The women themselves expect 1500 to 3000 Baht for sex. Supposedly the ladyboys sometimes go for less.

Both Nana Plaza and Soi Cowboy are come to a few short time hotels that rent out rooms by the hour. They are busy places.

Patpong was once the most well known bar district in Bangkok. Today it's not nearly as popular. Some legendary bars like Club Electric Blue have even shut down in recent years. Still many bars remain.

The Patpong bars are spread along Patpong Soi 1 and Patpong Soi 2. Nude dancing is not common in these bars. Coyote dancers are. There are also several ladyboy bars and some bars where ladyboys and natural born women co-mingle on stage.

Bar fines in Patpong range from 600 to 1000 Baht. A few bars used to have private quarters on premises but those seem to have gone the way of the dodo bird.

There are many blow job bars in Bangkok. Some have private rooms, others have curtained off couches. Staff in a few older bars still do the blow jobs right out in the open in front of other staff and customers.

Thanks to the internet the most known blow job bar in Bangkok is undoubtedly Wood Bar on Sukhumvit Soi 7/1. Other bars include Kasalong on Sukhumvit Soi 6, 7 Heaven on Sukhumvit Soi 33, and Rose Bar on Patpong Soi 1. Prices range from 700 to 1000 Baht.

There are only a few fetish bars in Bangkok. The most obvious is Bar Bar on Patpong Soi 2. The place looks like a dungeon inside and is staffed with women in skimpy outfits.

Escorts in Bangkok are common. They increasingly rely on the internet to find customers. Some use dating sites while others use purpose-made websites like the relatively new Smooci to find customers.

There are many soapy massage parlors in Bangkok. They range from the worn down to the luxury places that look like five star hotels. Many are located around Huay Kwang.

The women in these places either wait behind glass for customers or sit on the side near the customers. The latter are called "side-liners"

Services usually involve bathing, oral sex and condom covered intercourse. Prices range from 1,500 to 10,000 Baht. Most women charge something in between.

Soapy massage parlors have always catered to local guys and other Asians. Foreigners are accepted but sometimes charged an additional fee.

Recently a number of soapy massage parlors closed. Some were raided and shut down for breaking various laws. Others seem to have just gone out of business.

Annie's was one of the most well known sex shops in Thailand for many years. After 48 years of doing business it shut down in early 2018.

While soapy massage parlors are on the decline, the number of oily massage parlors in Bangkok seems to grow every day.

Oily massage parlors come in many shapes and sizes but they all follow a similar routine. Customers select a provider from a line up or photo book. Then they go to a private room where they're washed. Next they get a blow job and full service.

Oily massage parlors now offer various services and options including things like costumes and threesomes but the base prices are pretty much the same across the city. Customers normally pay 1900 to 2000 Baht for a session with sex.

The biggest concentrations of oily massage parlors are found on Sukhumvit Soi 22 and Sukhumvit Soi 24/1. Many other parlors can be found on Sukhumvit Soi 33 and in other parts of the city.

Freelancers in Bangkok have many avenues open to them. Many now use the internet to find customers. Others go to nightclubs like Insomnia at night. Still others stick to the old reliable method of working the street.

Street walkers can be found all over the main Sukhumvit strip day and night. Some also work Sukhumvit Soi 3 and Soi 4. Russians, Africans and eve Arab women can often be found among the many Thai ladies and ladyboys who work the streets for money. Sex is usually sold for 1000 to 1500 Baht.

Not far from Bangkok, the beach city of Pattaya is very much oriented towards the sex industry. Although some officials have announced that the place will be turned into a family friendly resort the truth is that Pattaya is still filled with sex workers from one end to the other.

Pattaya has all the venues you would expect, plus so-called gentlemen's clubs and an area called Bush Hill.

Go go bars are spread all over the city but the two main

areas where they are located are LK Metro and Walking Street.

Walking Street is the most well known part of the city. It's a long street lined with go go bars. Nowadays it's also filled with tourists including huge groups of Chinese and Korean people who photograph and video everything in sight.

Go go bars on Walking Street tend to be the most expensive in the country. Few have any nudity on display inside. Coyote dancers are common. Bar fines can be as much as 2000 Baht. Still the bars are busy. Walking Street ladies ask for anywhere from 2000 to 8000 Baht for sex depending on their popularity and other things.

On smaller streets connected to Walking Street bars are typically more open and less expensive. Topless women, nudity, and even the occasional blow jobs are all somewhat common. Bar fines are still around 600 Baht. Women usually want between 1500 and 3000 Baht for sex.

LK Metro is a street shaped like the letter L. It is much newer than Walking Street. There are several go go bars there. Some have women who dance topless. Most are in bikinis. Bar fines are usually 600 Baht. The women ask for anywhere between 1500 and 3000 Baht for sex.

Beer bars can be found all over the city. They're staffed by women who drink with men who buy them lady drinks. Most of them have sex with customers too. Bar fines are usually 600 Baht. The women usually want 1000 to 1500 Baht for sex.

The Devil's Den on Soi LK Metro is a somewhat unique place that specializes in "the porn star experience." It is loosely based on a similar place called the Eden Club in Bangkok.

When customers enter the Devil's Den the ladies on staff line up along the wall of the bar. There is a yellow line on the wall. Women on one side of the line do anal. Women on the other side do not. Services take place either in attached rooms with mirrors walls and ceilings, dildos, sex swings and televisions playing porn, or in the private hotel rooms of customers. Couples often visit the Devil's Den together. All of the women on staff are said to be genuinely bisexual. Customers take a minimum of two women at the Devil's Den. Prices start at 4000 Baht for 1 hour.

There are several soapy massage parlors in Pattaya. They are all quite large and have many women on staff. The most well known are Rasputin, Sabai Dee and Honey 2. The price for bathing, a blow job and full service sex in these places is anywhere from 2000 to 3000 Baht

Oily massage parlors aren't as common in Pattaya as they are in Bangkok, but there are still plenty around. Sex is normally included with sessions that cost 2000 Baht. Soi Honey is home to quite a few of these massage parlor. Others can be found on Soi Bukhao and in other parts of the city.

Regular Thai massage parlors abound too. They are all over the city. Some of them are totally non-sexual, but the simple fact is that in Pattaya even a number of the masseuses in the mainstream style massage parlors offer hand jobs and more to customers for tips of 500 to 1000 Baht once they are in private.

The infamous Soi 6 is lined from one end to the other with short time bars. The hundreds of scantly clad women who work these bars spend most of their time in the street trying to find customers. Lady drinks are sold inside but the women are not too insistent on getting them. The many money maker is sex. Customers usually pay 1300 Baht ($40 USD) for sex in the many rooms located above the bars. In some places on Soi 6 customers can get blow jobs right in the bars for 700 Baht ($22 USD).

Pattaya has its share of blow job bars too. Each has several women on staff. Oral sex is provided in semi-private areas or totally private rooms. Prices range from 600 to 800 Baht.

Unique to Pattaya are the gentlemen's clubs. These are

basically short time bars with locked doors. Customers ring bells outside to be let in. Inside the women on staff interact with customers often sexually. Services are rendered in the club, either right in the open, in semi-private booths, or in totally private rooms. Sex is sold for 1000 Baht.

Freelancers can be found all over the city. Many use the internet to find customers. Others go to night clubs. Still many more stand on Beach Road waiting to meet guys. Beach Road is such a common meeting place for sex workers and customers that it is jokingly called "the Coconut Bar." Freelancers usually ask for between 1000 and 2000 Baht for sex. Women on beach road ask for between 500 and 1000.

Finally there's "Bush Mountain." This dirty hill is lined with tattered shacks where women sell oral or full sex to customers for as little as 200 Baht.

The mountain city of Chiang Mai isn't known for its commercial sex industry but many people there sell sexual services every day.

There three go go bars in the city. None of them are very popular though they do get visitors. Nudity is uncommon. Most women wear panties and bras. The bar fines are usually 600 Baht. The dancers typically want 1500 Baht or more for sex.

There are many beer bars on Loi Kroh Road. They open around dark and are mostly staffed by middle aged women from the Isaan area. Bar fines are 500 Baht. The women want 1000 to 2000 Baht for sex.

Loi Kroh and roads around it are also filled with Thai massage parlors. As the attractive women posted in front of these places make clear, most also offer happy endings. Massages are 200 or 300 Baht. Hand jobs are 500 Baht more in most cases.

Thai massage parlors around the rest of the city sometimes have women who do happy endings. Others do not. It depends on the place and the providers themselves.

Other kinds of massage parlors oriented towards sexual services abound. Some like Raspberry are basically oily massage parlors. Others like Anime specialize in hand jobs. Prices range from 500 to 2000 Baht.

Chiang Mai has several soapy massage parlors too including the well known Sayuri Complex. These soapy massage parlors operate like those in Bangkok and Pattaya. They are mostly visited by Thai and other Asian guys. Westerners are only occasionally seen inside. Sessions cost between 1300 and 5000 Baht ($40-153 USD).

Thai and Asian customers are also the most common customers in the city's many Karaoke clubs. These places are staffed largely by tall, slim, white skinned Chiang Mai women who are famous for their beauty. Some of the Karaoke clubs have become infamous for padding bills and even ripping customers off entirely. Women in the clubs often have sex with customers. They ask for various sums of money depending on any number of factors.

A few brothels staffed mainly by women from ethnic minorities and immigrants from Burma can be found in Chiang Mai. The customer base is almost entirely locals and immigrant laborers. The price for sex is 500 Baht.

There aren't many escorts in Chiang Mai for whatever reason. There are more freelancers. Some work clubs like Zoe in Yellow looking for customers while others work the streets around Thapae Gate. Most do not seem to use the internet.

Another well known city with a big sex industry is Phuket, but even smaller towns like Hua Hin have some beer bars, brothels, nightclubs and soapy massage parlors. In many areas locals are the most common customers.

11. Vietnam

Vietnam is one of the largest countries in the world by population. It isn't well known for its sex industry but there are many sex workers in the countries. By some estimates there are actually millions.

Locals know this very well. It's not uncommon to hear them joke about places like *caphe om*s. Korean, Chinese and Japanese businessmen know it well too, as they are frequent customers. Western people don't seem to be aware by and large, perhaps because they expect to see go go bars or believe the country is similar to North Korea. While prostitution is illegal in Vietnam but it is also prevalent.

The most common venue where sex services are offered in the country is undoubtedly the massage parlor. There aren't as many regular massage parlors in Vietnam as there are in Cambodia or Thailand, but they do exist. Some of the women in those places offer sensual services for tips of 500,000 Dong ($22 USD) or so. Others do not.

Men's spas located in three star hotels are also common. They staff good looking women usually in their twenties who wear tight fighting skirts and low cut tops. They bathe and massage customers as a part of the regular service. Hand jobs are normally offered for tips of 200,000 to 500,000 Dong. Some also offer blow jobs.

In Ho Chi Minh City and Hanoi things usually go no further than a hand job in these sorts of places. But for whatever reason, full sex is commonly offered in similar venues in cities like Nha Trang.

In most of the country, full sex is most commonly sold by escorts and freelancers. The escorts work for agencies that don't publicize themselves. Instead the managers pretend to be individual women on websites and smart-phone apps then dispatch staff members to the rooms of the people they connect with for around 1,000,000 Dong ($44 USD). Freelancers hang around parks, ride motorbikes or visit nightclubs like Apocalypse Now in Ho Chi Minh City. Those found outside usually ask for a million Dong while those in nightclubs usually ask for $100 US Dollars.

There are also brothels that sometimes pretend to be barbershops where full sex is sold. Several are located near the airport in Saigon. They move all the time, probably to avoid law enforcement. They typically charge 500,000 to 1,000,000 Dong for bathing, a blow job and full sex.

More common are the blow job barbershops described earlier. Ho Chi Minh City has the most but they can be found in other cities too. Under the rubric of offering hair washing these places have women on staff who get topless or nude and perform oral sex. The normal price is around 300,000 Dong which includes a 200,000 Dong house fee. For whatever reason, Benny's in Saigon has become one of the most widely known shops of this type.

Other similar but less common shops are caphe om and *bia om*. These places look like local coffee shops and bars, and indeed they often are. What sets them apart are that the women on staff do anything from lap dances to blow jobs for customers when given a tip of 100,000 to 200,00 Dong.

There are also sexy cafes. Those are coffee shops staffed by attractive women in revealing clothes. The women sit and talk with customers but don't as a matter of course have sex for money. At most they may have attractive women in bikinis working as a "DJ." Some sexy beer bars follow a similar model.

Finally there are the hostess bars. Ho Chi Minh City is home to most of these places which cater to foreigners.

For years most hostess bars were centered on the Hai Ba

Trung thoroughfare. Most of them had names that indicated their addressed. So "49" was located at 49 Hai Ba Trung.

In the past the hostess bars mainly operated a lot like brothels. When customers entered the women on staff would line up. Customers would select a lady and buy a lady drink for her. Soon after they would either leave and give the lady a tip for her time or take the lady out of the bar to have sex in a nearby hotel for around 1,000,000 Dong. Those bars are mostly gone thanks in part due to a major crackdown. At most there are now one or two similar bars staffed mainly with older women where customers are offered oral sex or occasionally more in the bars themselves are rates as high as $100 USD.

Hostess bars are now more common then ever in Ho Chi Minh City but the current model rarely involves sex. Instead these hostess bars staff mainly attractive women in tight dresses who simply spend time and talk with customers. The customers buy them lady drinks for their time. As a general rule the women do not have sex with customers though some meet guys they come to know after hours for money. These kinds of hostess bars are located on Hai Ba Trung and nearby streets like Thi Sach.

Sex is often on offer in another smaller string of hostess bars along the Bui Vien backpacker street in Saigon. There the women on staff often seem keen to go out of the bar with customers for 2,000,000 Dong. They typically have sex with guys who pay this in nearby short time hotel rooms.

Gay prostitutes are also common in the area. They cruise up and down the street with noise makers as a semi-discrete way to advertise their availability.

12. Laos

Laos is between Thailand and Vietnam, both literally and figuratively. The sale of sexual services in Laos is relatively common but there is no abundance of commercial sex venues. It could hardly be otherwise in a country with such a low population, and population density.

Sex is sold in most towns and cities in Laos. In most cases Lao women offer sexual services but in others Vietnamese women are on staff.

In the capital city of Vientiane it is common for masseuses in regular massage parlors to offer customers hand jobs or blow jobs for 200,000 Kip ($24 USD). Occasionally full sex is even offered discreetly.

There is at least one massage parlor oriented towards sex entirely. It operates like a soapy massage parlor but there is no "fish bowl" display area. Customers simply get whoever is next in line.

The staff are all Vietnamese. They do 1 hour sessions that include bathing, massage, oral and full sex for 300,000 Kip ($36 USD).

Various hotels have fishbowl type setups inside. Customers can select women on staff for sex either in the hotel or somewhere else.

Freelancers in town usually meet their clients at the rooftop bar called Bor Pennyang or later at the nightclub called "At Home." They typically charge 200,000 to 800,000 Kip.

There are a few street walkers in Vientiane too. Most of them seem to be ladyboys. They are often found near the fountain in the middle of town. They charge 200,000 to 400,000

Kip.

In other parts of the country such as Luang Prabang and Vang Vieng women usually sell sexual services through massage parlors, brothels or Karaoke parlors. Prices for sex are between 200,000 and 500,000 Kip most times.

13. Cambodia

Also situated between Thailand and Vietnam, Cambodia has more than twice as many people as Laos. Fittingly it also has a much larger sex industry.

Sex and sexual services are sold all over Cambodia. Cambodian men are the main customer base; according to some estimates Cambodian men use prostitutes more than the men of any other country in the world. Of course there are also many other patrons of the sex industry in Cambodia including Chinese, African and Western men.

The most common venue for commercial sex in Cambodia is the brothel. They can be found all over the country including in small rural towns. In some places these run down brothels are referred to as "chicken farms." Sex is usually sold in these brothels for around $10 US dollars.

Phnom Penh is the largest city in the country. It is also home the largest percentage of rich people and foreigners. Sex work has more variation there than anywhere else in the country.

The most visible aspect of the local sex industry in Phnom Penh is the hostess bar. Years ago there were only a few hostess bars. Some of them were quite open with women on staff giving oral sex samples to guys who gave them a dollar. The wildest bars were all shuttered and a more subdued format took over.

New hostess bars are now opening left and right in Phnom Penh. In some a wild atmosphere is reemerging complete with scantly clad women dancing on tables, a practice long considered banned.

In the many hostess bars of Phnom Penh women in a mix of street clothes and dresses spend time with customers in exchange for lady drinks. Some of the women do not leave with customers at any time. Others leave with any man who asks them. Most are somewhere in between and only go to a hotel or other room for sex with a customer if they feel comfortable.

Hostess bars in Phnom Penh can be found on Street 51, Street 104, Street 108, Street 110, Street 118, Street 130, Street 136, Street 144, Street 172, and other areas. Bar fines are between $10 and $15 US. The women themselves want $30 to $100 for sex.

At least five fish bowl style massage parlors exist in Cambodia. Some are brightly lit with neon lights while others are discreetly tucked into the top floors of hotels. Most staff a mix of Cambodian and Vietnamese women. Prices are usually $6 to $10 for a session. The women ask $30 to $100 for sex.

There are many regular massage parlors in Phnom Penh too. They range from the small and run down to the large and elaborate. Erotic services are provided in many of the smaller places but not many of the larger ones. Many individual masseuses offer hand jobs and occasionally blow jobs or even full sex to male customers to get money. Prices asked range from $5 to $50.

Brothels are becoming less common in Phnom Penh but they certainly still exist. Many are now operating on the outskirts of the city. Some coffee shops double as brothels too. The women working in these places often hail from Vietnam. The prices charged for sex range from $5 to $25.

Freelancers are a common site at nightclubs like Pontoon and to a lesser extent at open air bars in the infamous Golden Sorya Mall. They charge their mostly foreign customers anywhere from $10 to $50 for sex.

Other women work more upscale places like the Darlin Darlin nightclub attached to the Nagaworld Casino and the Casa nightclub near Wat Phnom. They tend to ask for $100 or more for sex.

Escorts are not common in Cambodia. A few women use websites and applications to find customers but they aren't very common either. Street walkers on the riverside and around the Wat Phnom roundabout mostly work with local guys. They ask between $5 and $20 for sex.

Ladyboys were not very common a few years ago. Today many are seen selling sex in hostess bars and on the streets Ladyboys have existed for a long time in Cambodia however. The Thai word for ladyboys is kathoey which probably comes from Cambodia where the same word is used.

Siem Reap is home to the world famous Angkor Wat. There are no hostess bars in the city, but there are many sex workers. A few karaoke parlors staff women who sell sex. There are also some chicken farm style brothels. A few freelancers sell sex to customers in small local bars and nightclubs at night. Women often ask $100 for sex.

The beach city of Sihanoukville was long home to many hostess bars catering to foreigners. In recent years Chinese people have bought up much of the city and the hostess bars are now disappearing. Chinese massage parlors and brothels sometimes staffed by women from China are now becoming common.

Other cities like Kampot and Bavet have their share of karaoke parlors, brothels and small massage parlors where sex is sold somewhat discreetly. Locals make up nearly all the customers though some foreigners visit these places too.

14. Singapore

The city-state of Singapore is commonly thought of as being one of the most repressive places in the world. This book is not about liberty in Singapore but it is a fact that the sale of sex is permitted in Singapore.

Legal prostitution takes place mainly in the many brothels of Geylang. There brothels set up in converted residences work somewhat like oily massage parlors in Thailand. Customers walk inside and select one of the available women. Then they go to a private room where they shower before receiving a blow job and full sex. The women are mainly from China with those in some brothels coming from Thailand. Some semi-decrepit brothels also staff Indian women. The women who work these brothels are checked regularly to make sure they are of legal age and free from sexually transmitted infections like HIV. Condoms are typically used for everything including oral. The price for a session in these brothels ranges from 50 to 200 Singapore Dollars ($36-146 USD).

Keong Saik Street in Chinatown is another area that houses a lot of shop house brothels. The prices are a little lower than Geylang and the quarters tend to be more run down. Other semi-official red light districts exist on Petain Road and Desker Road. These areas are more dated. Prices are as low as half the normal rate in Geylang but the women can be two to three times as old as the gals working over there.

Of course many sex workers go beyond the realm of the legal and regulated sex industry. Some are tolerated while others face pressures from law enforcement.

The women who work the streets of Geylang or set up make shift brothels in hotels in the area are technically in violation of the law. Because of that the many women from places like Vietnam and Indonesia who take this route quickly disappear from sight when a police patrol comes through the area. When the coast is clear they sell sex for 50 to 100 SGD.

Karaoke parlors exist too, including in the Geylang area. They work like KTVs anywhere else in Asia. Prices vary but are usually on the high side. Chinese guys are the most common customers.

Escorts operate alone and through agencies in Singapore. Rumor has it that the uber-rich of Singapore have people who arrange their sexual activities. All other customers usually find escorts online. Singapore has it's own version of 141 and there's also a very popular forum called Sammy Boy Forum where all sorts of service providers are discussed and reviewed. Rates for escorts are all over the place.

Freelancers tend to stick to a few well known haunts. Brix is an expensive cocktail bar in the basement of the Grand Hyatt Hotel. Brix opens in the evenings and draws a large crowd nearly every night. By eleven o'clock it can be tough to move around inside. Hundreds of freelance prostitutes mingle with dozens of men around the bar every day of the week. Most of the guys are Westerners in business or business casual clothing. Asian businessmen are also present in small numbers. The freelance prostitutes in the bar mainly hail from Vietnam but other Asian and former Soviet Bloc countries are also represented. One or two South American women can even find their way to Brix occasionally.

The women are usually in their late twenties or thirties and generally average in looks. More than a few have enhanced breasts. They typically ask for 300-1000 Singapore Dollars ($220-732 US) for a short session of sex.

Some of the women commonly found at Brix claim to be regular professionals who just show up occasionally to make some extra money. I have no way to confirm or refute this.

Orchard Towers is a set of buildings that houses low end retail shops, homes and some bars that is often referred to as the "four floors of whores." During the day the public area looks like any other low rent mall in Asia with the exception of the small massage parlors scattered around. At night the stores shutter and a number of hostess bars open up to a small stream of mostly foreign customers. Some of the bars staff women and others simply attract freelancers. At least two of the bars have professional dancers and one only employs Thai ladyboys.

Women from the Philippines and Vietnam are most commonly found in these bars, but Thai, Ukrainian and Chinese gals are also seen with regularity. The women make money through salaries, lady drinks, the sale of sex, or a combination of all of the above. Not all of the women will leave with customers. Some are simply out to make tips.

Women who sell sex out of Orchard Towards can ask for anywhere from 200 to 500 Singapore Dollars ($146-366 US) for a roll in the hay. The small massage parlors scattered throughout the building offer half hour massages with hands on happy endings for 100 Singapore dollars ($80 US) all in. Some ladies and ladyboys can be found in the streets in front of the entrance every night. They typically ask for less than the women in the bars.

15. Burma

Prostitution is illegal in Burma. Still it is practiced widely. Sex is rarely sold in the open however, even when people know it's going on.

Yangon is no longer the capital of Burma, but it is still the largest city. It also has probably the largest local sex industry.

Although there were once strict rules in place against nightclubs in Yangon they were repealed years ago allowing many places to spring up around the city. Some clubs have reportedly been closed again recently and with all the changes going on in Burma there is no way to tell what will happen next.

Burma is home to a unique type of venue called a fashion club. Fashion clubs like Emperor and JJ's are probably the most popular adult entertainment venues for foreigners in Yangon even though the places were clearly designed for locals with money. They are not the only clubs of this type in town.

Fashion clubs aren't like the nightclubs one finds in most of the world. For the most part men sit around and drink and women try to find customers. Numerous freelancers walk around all night while trying to induce a customer to pick them up for a short romp while women considered by many to be of a higher level travel around in groups performing "fashion shows" each night. While these faux fashion models who number in the dozens walk up and down imaginary runways to loud music guys in the audience buy large flowered necklaces to show their affection by handing money to someone on staff. The women will sit with whoever buys them flowers after their performance and during this time many will negotiate for some sexually activities together off premises. A normal price for sex in these places is 100,000 Kyat ($65 USD) though popular women can ask for much more.

Nightclubs of the variety more common to the rest of the world also exist. As is the case in other Southeast Asian cities like Bangkok, Vientiane, and Phnom Penh, working women often prowl these clubs looking for customers. That is not to say that every woman in every club is working. Far from it, especially in Yangon. Some of the most popular nightclubs in the former capital include DJ Bar and GTR.

Karaoke establishments of the type popular all over Asia also exist in Myanmar. These places are catered toward locals and Asian businessmen. There are women working these places who provide company for customers who book a room for a period of time. They do things like sing and perhaps serve alcohol. Some will also join customers outside if they make them the right offer. One of the largest karaoke places in the city is the 5 story Asia Entertainment City complex which is directly across from the aforementioned JJ's.

Brothels are scattered all over the city and are the main haunts of local guys on low salaries who want to get their rocks off with no questions asked. These places are all unofficial and unadvertised and many work under the cover of other businesses.

The average Yangon brothel is in a worn down hotel with small rooms and smaller dirty beds on the floor where women provide a very limited version of full service as quickly as possible. Customers usually pay about 20,000 to 30,000 Kyat ($12-20 USD) for sex.

Street workers provide their services for even less than brothel workers. For the most part they target locals including the long distance truckers who seem to be their main client base. Ladyboys often mix in with the natural born females who walk the streets.

Regular bars are also around though they are few and far

between. Working women only appear to visit a few regularly. One is located in the Park Royal Hotel. There are no set fees as is the case with any set of self employed people though the average asking rate for sex seems to be about 100 US dollars or the equivalent in local currency.

Another bar where working women often show up on weekends is on the second floor of the five star Sule Shangri-La hotel which was long known as the Trader's Hotel. The women there ask for similar rates to their cohorts at the Park Royal bar which they are very likely also familiar with.

Sex is sold in other parts of Burma too. In most cases this is limited to street walkers, discreet brothels, and occasionally a bar or nightclub, with a few notable exceptions. Most customers are locals or visiting Asian businessmen.

16. Indonesia

Indonesia is described as the largest Muslim country in the world. Prostitution is officially outlawed yet sexual services are offered all over the archipelago.

Jakarta is the capital and largest city in Indonesia. It's also home to a sizable Chinese population. Sex is sold in a variety of places in the city.

Compensated dating takes place with arrangements usually made through the internet. Dating sites and smart-phone applications are used and rates paid vary from one person to the next.

Bars and clubs are more specific venues for paid pick ups. Many of them either hire working women or attract freelance working women looking for customers.

Night clubs are often filled with prostitutes. Some may work for the club owners while others are simply freelancers. Interestingly in Jakarta prostitutes and "regular girls" often go to the same clubs without issue. Rates vary so much from one woman to the next that it's impossible to give anything approaching an average.

A few lounge style bars are known for attracting the same kinds of freelancers that can be found in the aforementioned BRIX in Singapore. B.A.T.S. at the Hotel Shangri-La is a very popular place that is filled with working women from around the world every night of the week. CJ's in the Hotel Mulia Senayan and Tiga Puluh in Hotel Le Meridien are similar establishments. Women working these bars tend to ask for a lot more than women in other places around the city.

Adult entertainment complexes offer all sorts of options

under one large roof. They occupy entire buildings and staff dozens or even hundreds of people. These places are large and usually quite obvious. They normally contain night clubs, karaoke rooms, therapeutic massage areas and spas with women offering full service sex in the guise of massage. Many also feature sexy women dancing in various states of undress.

Full service massage can typically be had for anywhere from 325,000 Rupiah ($22 USD) to more than 1,500,000 Rupiah ($1o3 USD) depending on the lady and the venue. Foreign women from places like China and Russia tend to get higher rates than locals with the exception of the sexy dancers.

Although the entertainment complexes are known and popular they are not without their critics. The new government of Jakarta actually moved to closed the spa in the infamous Alexa hotel over claims of prostitution. Only time can tell what will happen with these kinds of places in the future.

Jakarta's Blok M area contains a small strip of bars where freelancers congregate and a few staff dancers work poles on stage. Most Blok M bars attract foreigners who the working women in the area target. Prices for sex range from 300,000 to 1,200,000 Rupiah ($20-82 USD). The most notable place in the area is probably D's Place with its small gogo-like stage for dancing girls and secret room.

Blok M is also home to a number of karaoke parlors aimed at Japanese customers. These places recently made the news when basketball players from Japan were said to have visited during the Asia Games.

Massage parlors also abound in Jakarta. They aren't as plentiful as they are in Thailand but they definitely exist. Some are mainstream but many offer happy endings or full service as a part of the regular program. Popular places include Sumo Spa and Kimochi. The price for a massage and sex is usually around 350,000 Rupiah ($24 USD).

Street walkers can be found in various areas of the

Jakarta at night. Jalan Hayam Wuruk seems to be popular for this at times. Prices are as low as one might expect.

Red light districts exist in the city. Kalijodo is one of the oldest and most well known. Bongkaran is another. Short time sessions are sold to locals for as little as 50,000 Rupiah ($3 US).

The very rich in Jakarta have their own world of private parties and clubs. They've been variously reported in the media in the past. None are open to the public.

Sex is commonly sold in Surabaya and Bali too. Massage parlors are common and there are red light districts but recently the internet has become the most popular place to sell sex.

Smart-phone applications, dating sites and even mainstream social media is filled with profiles advertising massage parlors and spas. Many of these are thinly-veiled advertisements for prostitution. Some of the profiles are fakes designed to scam guys out of their money.

In the rest of Indonesia sex is usually sold through brothels though there are some clubs and increasingly women and agencies who rely on the internet to find customers.

17. Kenya

Sex work is legal in some parts of Africa and outlawed in others. Regardless, it flourishes throughout the continent. There is perhaps no better example of the commercial sex scene in African than Kenya.

There are many professional and part-time sex workers in Kenya. The largest numbers can be found in the cities of Nairobi and Mombasa. There is no national law against sex work but some cities prohibit it. Still the practice is widespread.

The internet is now one of the most common ways for sex workers to find customers in Kenya. Others stick to well known bars. Freelancers of this sort usually ask 2000 to 4000 Shillings ($20-40 USD) for sex.

Escorts use the internet almost exclusively. Some are from Kenya but others from various parts of the world also ply their trade in the country. Prices can vary quite a bit.

Happy ending massage isn't common but there are a few massage parlors in Nairobi where women sell hand jobs or full sex. Full service goes for around 8000 Shillings ($80 USD).

Brothels in Kenya aren't as common as they used to be. The places that still exist tend to be in run down and dangerous areas. Local customers who venture into these brothels pay as little as 500 Shillings ($5 USD) for sex.

18. Costa Rica

Prostitution is legal in Costa Rica with some stipulations. The exacts of the law and the actual practice are often in conflict. It is the same story told around the world.

The sale of sexual services is common in Costa Rica. It is probably most common in the capital city of San Jose.

Several bars in San Jose like the well known Blue Marlin are common stomping grounds for freelance prostitutes. Some of these women are locals but others from countries like Colombia, Venezuela and the Dominican Republic also work the circuit. Sex is commonly sold for $50 to $100 US dollars.

San Jose and the rest of the country is also home to an assortment of strip clubs, bars and avenues known for street walkers. Prices can vary greatly. Most customers are local but foreigners also visit some of these places with regularity.

19. Nicaragua

Nicaragua borders Costa Rica. Prostitution is also legal in Nicaragua and probably just as common. Perhaps because Nicaragua is much poorer, the average rates for sex in Nicaragua are lower than those across the border.

Prostitution in Nicaragua takes on a variety of forms. The capital city Managua has them all. There are several strip clubs along with many bars where sex workers are known to congregate. There are also certain public areas that are known for street walkers. Perhaps most common of all are the short time bars like Fenix.

Fenix is a big place that seems to be permanently under construction. Every few months sees another expansion. Inside there are televisions playing porno, a small bar, lots of tables and chairs, and plenty of working girls sitting around.

Customers at Fenix usually hang around and drink in between sessions. When they want sex they simply negotiate with one of the women in the bar. The average price for sex in the one of the private rooms in back is 600 Cordobas ($19 USD).

Other bars operate on similar lines. Outside of Managua the prices for sex are often even lower.

20. The Dominican Republic

Prostitution is legal in the Dominican Republic. It's also common. Some small towns like Sosua and Boca Rica have even become world famous for their local commercial sex industries.

The law officially prohibits things like brothels. The many brothels around the country aimed at locals where sex is sold for as little as 700 Pesos ($15 USD) continue to operate but several places frequented by foreigners in towns like Sosua have been shut down. In those areas sex workers have simply moved into the streets and open air bars. Some even ply their trade on the beach.

Independent sex workers who meet customers outside or over the internet tend to charge between 1500 and 3000 Pesos ($30-60 USD) for sex.

Massage parlors aren't too common but they do exist in some numbers. Several massage parlors in Sosua staffed by Haitian women charge 1000 Pesos ($20 USD) for a massage with a hand job happy ending.

A handful of all-inclusive places remain in the area around Sosua seemingly without problem. These are basically closed off resorts where guys have sex with women who show up regularly for several thousand Pesos.

Other cities have dance clubs and even car washes where women sell sex. Most customers are locals. The price for a blow job and intercourse is usually between 1000 and 2000 Pesos.

21. Panama

Prostitution is legal in Panama. There are several brothels and happy ending massage parlors in the country. There are also several bars that are known freelancer haunts.

Places like Habano's Cafe in Panama city fill up with sex workers every night of the week. On most nights the women outnumber the male customers twenty or thirty to one.

In Panama the US dollar is accepted along with the local currency as a general practice. Sex workers accept both too. The ladies at places like Habano's who hail from Panama as well as Colombia, the Dominican Republic, Venezuela and even Cuba, usually ask $150 dollars for sex.

The women who work as escorts can ask for the same amount or more depending on any number of factors. Ladies who work casino floors for customers tend to ask for something closer to $100.

22. Colombia

Panama and Colombia were once part of the same country. Perhaps its no coincidence then that prostitution is also legal in Colombia. The sale of sex is probably even more widespread in Colombia than it is in Panama. At the very least the prices are generally much lower.

The sale of sex is common all across Colombia. While each city's commercial sex scene can have its own peculiarities, prices are pretty similar all around.

In Bogota, bars and sex clubs are common. The bars like Lalo's are set up somewhat like strip clubs though women do rarely dance and never take off their clothes. Guys can purchase lady drinks and talk with the ladies or take them away for sex at a cost of around 200,000-300,000 pesos ($67-100 USD). That comes on top of a bar fine that costs 185,000 pesos ($62 USD). At sex clubs like Loutron men have sex with women in the line up for 300,000 pesos ($101 USD).

There are also less expensive places. In the Santa Fe red light district women sell sex out of small rooms for 30,000 Pesos ($10 USD).

In Medellin, strip clubs and brothels are more common. At the strip clubs women work the stages in revealing clothes and have sex with customers who request it. Prices range from 80,000 to 190,000 Pesos ($26-64 USD) depending on the place. At the brothels which are basically low rent versions of the Bogota sex clubs a session including oral and intercourse costs around 40,000 Pesos ($13 USD).

Medellin is also home to some massage parlors where one hour sessions including oral and full sex are sold for 150,000 Pesos ($50 USD).

Street walkers can be found across Colombia. They are often desperate and thus accepting of very low amounts of money for oral sex or intercourse.

23. Mexico

Mexico is home to many brothels and various other commercial sex venues. One commentator says "they are about as difficult to find as sand on a beach."

Brothels are probably the most common venues for the sale of sex in Mexico, but strip clubs also abound. Tijuana is for sure the most known part of the country when it comes to sex. The town contains several strip clubs where sex is sold openly.

Just across the border from San Diego, California, Tijuana is home to places like Hong Kong and Adelita's where nude dancers on stage have intercourse with customers on a regular basis. Lap dances are available for $20 but many customers go further than that.

The prices for sex in these kinds of places are negotiable. The women do their best to get customers excited so they can propose higher fees but the standard still remains at between $50 and $80 US. Sex is usually done quickly in nearby rooms and often doesn't include oral sex or changes in positions. Customers normally include the types of services they want in their negotiations before paying.

Tijuana also has its share of street walkers including a few ladyboys. Prices vary from as little as $15 USD to as much as $50 USD.

In other parts of the country sex is usually cheaper. There are exceptions. Escorts with light skin in Mexico City for example can sometimes charge rates that rival those of so-called high end escorts in New York.

24. Germany

As with many things, Europe has a divided approach to prostitution. In some countries it is illegal. In others it is permitted. In all countries it exists.

Prostitution is legal in Germany and the nearby countries where German is commonly spoken. Across Germany there are countless escorts, independent sex workers and street walkers who charge various rates.

There are also *laufhaus* apartment blocks filled with prostitutes who sell sex in a way that much resembles places like the aforementioned Fuji Building in Hong Kong. The Bahnhofsviertel in Frankfurt is one such place. Sex is sold there for 25 Euros ($29 USD) and up.

Another common model in Germany is the bordello style brothel. These are staffed by groups of women from Germany and other parts of the world who sell sex in sessions starting at 60 Euros ($70 USD).

On top of the brothels and apartment blocks filled with prostitutes there are also the previously described FKK sex saunas. These are probably the most well known types of commercial sex venues in the country.

In Berlin the only really notable FKK is Artemis. The smaller city of Frankfurt on the other hand is home to many well-known FKK saunas including Oase and Mainhattan where sex is sold for 50 Euros a go. Still other cities are home to even more of these clubs, as are some other countries in Europe.

25. Austria

Austria borders Germany. It has similar laws in place too. Prostitution is permitted in various forms. Street walkers are somewhat common. Brothels aren't as common but they do exist, usually selling sex for 50 Euros or more.

Strip clubs like Maxim in Vienna have women on staff who make their money mainly by selling sex to customers for 120 Euros ($140 USD) per session or more.

At FKKs like the famous Goldentime in Vienna, sex is usually sold for 60 Euros per session. Farther from the capital in places like Wellcum Hotel and Sauna in Hohenthurn, sex is usually sold for 50 Euros per round.

26. Switzerland

Switzerland is home to many German speakers. It is also home to a lot of prostitution too!

Most universal forms of sex work can be found in Switzerland. The country has a high cost of living and the prices by sex workers usually correspond to that, but there are exceptions.

At bordello style brothels like Club Oceano in Lugano sex is usually sold at around 100 Euros per session. This seems to be a fairly average price for the country.

There are no blow job bars in Europe. According to reports one man recently planned to change that. His claims to be opening a blow job cafe were widely covered in the news but as of yet nothing seems to have come of it. For now the only blow job cafes remain in Vietnam.

Without a doubt the most notable aspect of the commercial sex industry in Vienna are the sex boxes built by the government in Zurich. These "boxes" are basically small open garages customers with cars can pull into after picking up a prostitute. Each box contains an emergency button for sex workers who run into problems but so far they have not seen much use at all.

The boxes are immensely popular among sex workers, their customers and even locals in Zurich. They have helped organize the local industry in a way that makes a lot of sense.

27. The Czech Republic

Prostitution is legal in the Czech Republic. It's also widespread. Still there are some gray and off limit areas. This is demonstrated by brothels that refuse to advertise their addresses and period raids of sex clubs.

Prague is the biggest city in the country and thus home to the largest local commercial sex scene. There are several venues in the city where sexual services as sold openly.

There is no glass window red light district in Prague but two market style businesses operate on a similar model. At both Showpark DaVinci and Showpark Market customers pay an entry fee for access to a closed building filled with sex workers who rent out rooms inside. Each place has a bar where customers and women meet and mingle. The price for sex is negotiable but most customers pay 1500 Koruna for a blow job and sex.

Many brothels are scattered around the city. They advertise online and typically only reveal their exact addresses to customers after they call. Most are set up in large apartments in residential buildings filled with people who may not enjoy the presence of such shops next door. Sessions usually involved oral sex and intercourse. Prices start at 800 Koruna ($36 USD).

In the city's strip clubs dancers are more likely to have sex with a customer than actually get nude on stage. Some places like AAA Exclusive Club look like American strip clubs inside. Others like K5 Relax look more like FKK sex saunas that just happen to have some stripper poles around. The rate for sex in a Czech strip club starts at between 2000 and 2400 Koruna ($90-108 USD).

Only one FKK style sex sauna exists in Prague. That's

Sexy Sauna Erotic Club. Located inside a historic looking building in the middle of Prague 1, the place is filled with nude women from around Europe. It is large and cavernous with showers, locker rooms, big lounges, and unique hanging pods where sex usually takes place. The women who work in the club typically charge 1900 Koruna ($86 USD) for a short session of covered oral and intercourse.

28. The Netherlands

The Netherlands is probably the most well known place for prostitution on the globe. The legal red light districts of Amsterdam are world famous. Prostitution in the country exists in other locations and forms too.

Through word of mouth and local and international tourist campaigns De Wallen has become a major tourist attraction in Amsterdam. In fact it may be the largest in the city if the throngs of people walking around every day are any indication. Couples stroll hand in hand down alleys lined with illuminated windows filled with half naked women offering sex for money. Somehow this feels natural in Amsterdam even though organized tours of Chinese and Korean people gawking at scantly clad dancers on Pattaya's Walking Street does not. Perhaps the level of public acceptance and mix of houses, sex museums and marijuana selling "coffee shops" in De Wallen has something to do with that. Perhaps the rules against people taking pictures of the women in De Wallen windows does too.

The history of the area is quite interesting. In the past things worked as they do today in some parts of Asia with sex workers plying their trade out of hair salons, massage parlors and gambling centers. Brothels and pimps were outlawed at one point but the sale of sex was not. At some point a health check system was enacted that required working women to produce a card showing they were free of disease. Eventually it all led to the current situation in which women work individually out of small rooms with large windows facing the street where they can advertise. The Museum of Prostitution in De Wallen does a good job of telling the story.

Although there is so much around the women in the

windows are still the center of attraction. Some ladies start working in the afternoon but the area really comes alive at night. EU citizenship or residency is required to work in De Wallen but women from all over the world ply their trade there. One estimate says that at least sixty percent of the women working the windows come from outside of the Netherlands. That seems to be true. Most of the women working in De Wallen hail from Eastern Europe. Ladies from other parts of Europe along with Asia, Africa and Latin America are also represented along with a fairly large number of transsexuals.

Customers who see a woman they like approach the window she works in. The woman will then open the door to allow for negotiations. Sex in De Wallen is purely a business transaction and most of the women who work there want to get the most money they can for the least amount of effort. If a customer negotiates twenty minutes of sex for 50 Euros ($55 USD) he will most likely get exactly what they said which is quick sex in one position and nothing more. Customers who want to change positions or receive oral sex normally need to say it up front. If they ask for it when in the room they may be asked for more money. Things like kissing are considered extras and usually require more money as well. Every activity is covered. Condoms are used for intercourse and oral sex as one might expect but they are also used in ways which could surprise unwitting customers. An example of that would be a sex worker rolling a condom over a customer's finger if he shells out money for the privilege of manipulating her vagina by hand.

Sexual services are provided in small rooms attached to the window displays. Curtains are drawn so that no one on the street can see what is going on inside.

The smaller Singelgebied and De Pijp red light districts work on the same model though they are generally less expensive and more popular among locals.

The Netherlands also has its share of street walkers.

Usually they are women who cannot get work permits for the windows.

There are also women who troll parks and porn theaters looking for customers along with happy ending massage parlors and private sex clubs that are more or less bordello style brothels behind locked doors.

V. Conclusion

As you can see, the world's oldest profession is also one of its most predominant. While I have not come close to reporting on each and every aspect of prostitution around the world, I hope I have succeeded in giving you a good idea of the kinds of things that go on in the adult service industry, both in general and in specific countries.

Again I must emphasize that I do not advocate violating any laws or participating in any adult activities. Each person has to make their own judgments and decisions. I've only described things as they actually are.

Your mileage may vary.

Disclaimer

The author does not advocate any illegal activities. In fact, he does not advocate anything at all. This book was written purely for educational and entertainment purposes. The reader assumes all risks and responsibilities for their own actions.

The facts are the facts. Those who can't deal with them might best be served by a cold shower or perhaps even some counseling.

The contents of this book are intended only as adult entertainment.

Also available from the Author:

Happy Ending Massage: The Complete Report

Blowjob Bars: The Complete Report

Prostitution in Berlin: The Complete Report

Prostitution in Taipei: The Complete Report

Prostitution in Frankfurt: The Complete Report

Prostitution in Vienna: The Complete Report

Prostitution in Macau: The Complete Report

Prostitution in Jakarta: The Complete Report

Sex Talk : Discussions with Prostitutes, Porn Stars, Producers, Photographers and Penmen

www.RockitReports.com